Words That Built a Nation

Voices of Democracy That Have Shaped America's History

Marilyn Miller, Ellen Scordato, and Dan Tucker
Illustrated by Mary Kate McDevitt

RODALE KiDS

RODALE KiDS
RODALEKIDS.COM

An imprint of Rodale Books
733 Third Avenue
New York, NY 10017
Visit us online at rodalekids.com

Portions of this book were previously published as *Words That Built a Nation: A Young Person's Collection of Historic American Documents* by Stonesong Press, LLC, in September, 1999.

This revised edition is published by Rodale Inc. by special arrangement with Stonesong Press, LLC.

Copyright © 2018, 1999 by Stonesong Press, LLC
Illustrations © Mary Kate McDevitt

Rodale Kids books may be purchased for business or promotional use or for special sales. For information, please e-mail: RodaleKids@Rodale.com.

Printed in China
Manufactured by RRD Asia 201801

Photo credits appear on page 224.
Interior design by Jessica Nordskog

Library of Congress Cataloging-in-Publication Data is on file with the publisher.

ISBN 978–1–63565–188–1   hardcover

Distributed to the trade by Macmillan

10 9 8 7 6 5 4 3 2 1   hardcover

For the next generation of Americans,
whose words and actions will continue
to build this nation.

CONTENTS

Introduction ∾ 6

INTRODUCTION

Every day, Americans look to a document that's well over two centuries old, written by men wearing breeches and using a quill pen, for guidance in making and enforcing the laws that govern our lives—down to the rules about the information our Internet providers are allowed collect about our Google searches. America's founders never could have foreseen the Internet, but somehow, the words and principles they lay down in the United States Constitution in 1787 remain as relevant today as they were when they were written.

The Constitution remains the basis for our government, but is only one of many documents that have shaped and defined the American character. This book looks at the words and ideas from forty-one of the most important documents and speeches in American history. These are words that capture the battles, the crises, the values, and the politics of a developing government. These words are living history, telling the story of a new nation whose destiny was far from certain—and which continues, in the twenty-first century, to unfold. The words in this book, compiled from speeches, pamphlets, letters, declarations, and even songs, represent the past, present, and future of our nation.

When the Mayflower left the shores of England in 1620, its passengers were seeking religious freedom and escape from the seemingly endless wars that were plaguing Europe at the time. They regarded the New World as virgin territory—although Native Americans had been living there for millenia. Some of the Europeans simply wanted better economic opportunity. The leaders on the Mayflower knew that with the king and English authority so distant, they would need a governing document if they were to succeed as a colony in the New World. Before they even touched land, they developed the compact that bound them together in obedience first to God and to the king—but most importantly for the American story, to each other. The authority of their government came from the consent of the governed, and the idea of self-government was planted on North American soil. So began the series of trials and errors that turned settlements into colonies, colonies into states, and states into a nation.

The Mayflower Compact and other documents connect our past to our present. Generations of Americans since then have developed, interpreted, and applied the concepts in these documents to changing events and social conditions. From the Declaration of Independence (1776), to the Declaration of Sentiments (1848), to the Declaration of Indian Purpose (1961), this country's sense of government, freedom, and citizenship runs through its veins and finds its expression in print.

Besides these cornerstone documents, many of the other documents chosen represent turning points in American history. Their existence altered the course,

or direction, of the nation by influencing popular opinion, or by giving expression to the evolving values of the American population. Afterward, the country and the people were forever changed. This was true of Frederick Douglass's account of his life as a slave, which informed a still-skeptical society of the horrors of slavery. Douglass's 1852 speech about the meaning of the Fourth of July to black Americans—most of whom were still enslaved—still reverberates today.

Some of the documents included here expanded the idea of citizenship by letting more voices be heard in our society. This was not done without struggle. In 1870, the Fifteenth Amendment secured the vote for African-American men. Fifty years later, in 1920, the approval of the Nineteenth Amendment gave women the same right. In 2015, the Supreme

> These documents make it clear that individual rights and the institutions of government and the rule of law must be nurtured and protected.

Court extended the guarantees of equal treatment under the law to same-sex couples in the landmark *Obergefell v. Hodges* decision.

The nation's expansion took economic forms as well. Although it began as a nation of farmers, the United States ultimately became a great industrial power. By the end of the nineteenth century, waves of immigrants searching for jobs entered the United States in greater numbers than before. Most of the newcomers settled in cities, where they added to the richness and diversity of American life. Included in this collection is a 1910 account by reformer Jane Addams of the poor conditions immigrants had to face. Indeed, as reformers like Addams tried to include newcomers in American life, prejudice against immigrants and minorities was widespread, and many Americans were concerned that immigrants would take their jobs away. In 1967, César Chávez's moving words to striking Mexican farmworkers in California gave notice that the question of immigrants' rights was far from resolved. Chavez's speech led to dramatically improved working and living conditions for thousands of immigrant workers.

The Civil Rights movement was perhaps the defining movement of U.S. history in the latter part of the twentieth century. In 1954, the Supreme Court ruled in *Brown v. the Board of Education* that segregated schools favored whites at the expense of blacks,

because black schools simply didn't get the resources that white schools did. The ruling overturned the idea of "separate but equal," which had been the law of the land, and which had allowed segregation to keep blacks from receiving opportunities for education and economic success equal to whites. Martin Luther King, Jr.'s 1963 "I Have a Dream' speech built upon this assertion and led inexorably to the passage of the Civil Rights Act in 1964—a crucial milestone in the ongoing struggle for blacks to gain equal treatment under the law. Barack Obama's speech on race, given when he was an Illinois senator campaigning for the presidency in 2008, provides a more recent picture of where that struggle stands.

Some words resound beyond a nation's borders. John F. Kennedy admitted in his speech at the Berlin Wall in Germany in 1963 that "freedom has many difficulties and democracy is not perfect," but, pointing to the poor conditions in which the Soviets were effectively imprisoning East German citizens with the wall, went on to say that "freedom is indivisible, and when one man is enslaved, all are not free." Just over two decades later, Ronald Reagan gave a rousing speech in the same location, signaling the end of the Cold War, just as surely as Kennedy's had marked its peak.

When Hillary Rodham Clinton spoke at the United Nations Conference on Women in Beijing, China, in 1995, she made the case that women's rights and human rights are one and the same thing, strengthening the bulwark for combating the oppression of women in many parts of the world—while also acknowledging the less-than-perfect record of the United States on the rights of women. In many ways, her speech owed its existence to the work and words of those who fought for women's right to vote, such as Lucretia Mott and Elizabeth Cady Stanton, in the 1800s.

The same words that govern the personal freedoms of America's citizens also define the United States to the rest of the world. Indeed, in the eyes of the Eastern bloc citizens who flocked to the West during and after the Cold War in the middle of the twentieth century, and from the point of view of civil rights activists in South Africa who fought against apartheid (a policy of total racial discrimination) America is freedom. To refugees from civil wars from the Sudan to Syria, the United States represents safety and prosperity. Our documents, our words inspire their actions, and this is why people from around the world flock to the United States to live, in many cases risking their lives just to get in, and frequently making great sacrifices, like living apart from family, just to stay.

Yet the state of the union is far from perfect. If anything, these documents make it clear that individual rights and the institutions of government and the rule of law must be nurtured and protected. The documents in this book will be interpreted and reinterpreted by each generation, including yours. There is no better way of protecting your own rights and interests than by understanding what they are, where they came from, and with your participation, where they are headed. ★

Senator Barack Obama, then a presidential hopeful, delivers a speech in 2007 at the Brown Chapel AME Church in Selma to commemorate the anniversary of "Bloody Sunday," the 1965 civil rights demonstration in that city that turned violent. Some of those listening to Obama had been present 42 years earlier, when state troopers used tear gas and batons to break up the otherwise peaceful protest as marchers crossed the Edmund Pettus Bridge. (See page 204)

THE MAYFLOWER COMPACT

November 11, 1620

After 65 days on rough seas, with 102 people aboard, the sailing ship *Mayflower* approached Cape Cod, Massachusetts. Storms and errors had forced the ship far off course from Virginia, its original destination. During the long voyage the passengers had overcome many crises. Now, exhausted and weakened by poor diet and illness, they faced a new challenge.

The "Pilgrims," as about 40 of the passengers became known, had received a charter allowing them to establish a colony in Virginia. Now they were about to build a colony far to the north,

where they had no legal right to settle. They realized that for their settlement to survive they must immediately agree on an orderly way to govern it. So, on November 11, 1620, 41 of the adult males on board signed an agreement called the Mayflower Compact.

They pledged to form a Christian government that would make just and equal laws on behalf of their community that the members of their settlement agreed to obey. The Mayflower Compact was the first document of self-government for North America.

THE MAYFLOWER COMPACT

In the name of God Amen. We whose names are under-written, the loyall subjects of our dread soveraigne Lord King James by the grace of God, of great Britaine, France, & Ireland king, defender of the faith, &c.

Haveing undertaken, for the glorie of God, and advancements of the Christian faith and honour of our king & countrie, a voyage to plant the first colonie in the Northerne parts of Virginia, doe by these presents solemnly & mutualy in the presence of God, and one of another, covenant & combine our selves togeather into a civill body politick; for our better ordering, & preservation & furtherance of the ends aforesaid; and by vertue hearof to enacte, constitute, and frame shuch just & equall lawes, ordinances. Acts, constitutions, & offices, from time to time, as shall be thought most meete & convenient for the general good of the Colonie: unto which we promise all due submission and obedience.

In witnes whereof we have hereunder subscribed our names at Cap-Codd the • 11 • of November, in the year the raigne of our soveraigne Lord King James of England, France, & Ireland, the eighteenth and of Scotland the fiftie fourth, An°: Dom. 1620.

Opposite page: Pilgrims gather around a table to sign the Mayflower Compact. The Compact was used to govern the settlement until Plymouth became part of the Massachusetts Bay Colony in 1691. The baby in the cradle, Peregrine White, was the first English baby born in New England. White was born on board the *Mayflower* on November 20, 1620, as the ship sailed off Cape Cod Harbor.

The colonists came ashore on December 26, 1620, at Plymouth. William Bradford, one of their leaders, later recalled that "the whole country, full of woods and thickets, represented a savage hue."

John Winthrop was the first governor of the Massachusetts Bay Colony, founded nine years after the Pilgrims landed in Plymouth, Massachusetts.

The *Mayflower's* exact specifications are lost to time, but it is known that the hand-built wooden ship was a galleon or carrack, square-rigged, and about 80 to 100 feet from stern (back) to bowsprit (the pointy thing on the front). The *Mayflower* was a merchant ship, not meant for passengers, so the Pilgrims' quarters were on the mid-level gun, or "tween" deck, which was only about 5½ feet in height. The ship had already seen a long life as a merchant vessel when the Pilgrims embarked in 1620 and was somewhat weather-beaten.

AUTHORS

There were 102 men and women aboard the *Mayflower*. The adult male signers did not include the servants and seamen. Women could not sign because they had no political rights. As was the case with nearly all European settlers' governing documents, no mention was made of Native Americans.

RESPONSE

The new colony was too small and too far away for a great European power such as England to pay attention to it. During town meetings the local colonial government relied on the authority given them in the Mayflower Compact to pass laws, elect assistants to the governor, and add new voters.

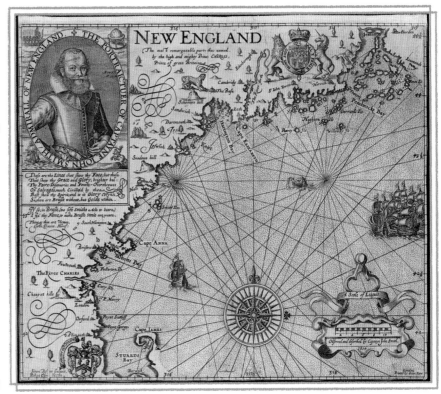

Explorer John Smith was one of the leaders of the English colony at Jamestown, Virginia. In 1614 he sailed along the northeast coast and in 1616 made this map of the region he named New England.

About 40 of the 102 passengers on the *Mayflower* were English Separatists—men and women who had separated themselves from the Church of England because they believed it was hopelessly corrupt. Most Separatists were farmers and craftworkers. The Separatists referred to themselves as "Saints," and by openly supporting a break with the Church of England, they were risking their lives.

The secular, or nonreligious, passengers on the *Mayflower* were called "Strangers." They joined the voyage for a variety of reasons—some for better economic opportunity, some to escape difficult family circumstances, still others to escape a criminal conviction.

EARLY to BED *and* EARLY to RISE

MAKES a MA[N] HEALTHY WEALTHY *and* WISE

POOR RICHARD'S ALMANACK

BENJAMIN FRANKLIN

1732 – 1758

Benjamin Franklin published this annual almanac in Philadelphia. It contained a calendar, weather predictions, recipes, medical advice, farming tips, and an astrological guide. Franklin also included Poor Richard's proverbs—brief, clever sayings related to daily life. These sayings reflected the value of hard work and common sense. The following proverbs are from Franklin's almanac.

Benjamin Franklin, at right, works as an apprentice in Boston in the printer's shop of his older brother James. During colonial times, apprentices training for a job did not receive a salary but did get food and lodging.

POOR RICHARD'S ALMANACK

- He that waits upon a Fortune, is never sure of a Dinner. Keep thy shop, and thy shop will keep thee.

- Three may keep a secret if two of them are dead.

- Early to bed and early to rise, makes a man healthy wealthy and wise.

- Diligence is the Mother of Good-Luck.

- Do not do that which you would not have known.

- Wealth is not his that has it, but his that enjoys it. God helps them that help themselves.

- Don't throw stones at your neighbours, if your own windows are glass. ★

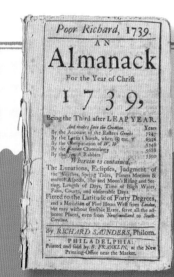

The cover of the first edition of Poor Richard's Almanack shows the author as "Richard Saunders," a pen name used by Ben Franklin.

AUTHOR

Benjamin Franklin (1706–1790), a coauthor and signer of both the Declaration of Independence and the Constitution, is considered one of the founding fathers of the United States—not bad for the self-educated son of a candle- and soap-maker. Franklin apprenticed as a young man to his brother, a printer, and later became a successful author, patriot, politician, diplomat, inventor, scientist, and philosopher. Born in Boston, Franklin abandoned his printing apprenticeship and moved to Philadelphia in 1723, where he began printing his own newspaper, books, and Poor Richard's Almanack. Franklin was so successful that he was able to give up active control of his printing business in 1848, when he was forty-two years old. For the rest of his life he devoted himself to other interests.

RESPONSE

Almanacs were extremely popular colonial reading matter. Of all the colonial almanacs, Franklin's is the best known, even though Franklin did not make up all the proverbs and sayings in Poor Richard's Almanack. He borrowed many from popular sayings and the Bible, often rewriting them. More colonists read Poor Richard's Almanack than any other publication except the Bible.

When he was twelve years old, Franklin began working for his brother James. Soon he was writing essays for James's newspapers. The young Franklin never signed his own name to these essays but used made-up names. This was a common practice in his day.

Franklin did not use his own name in publishing the almanac. Rather, he wrote under the fictional name of Richard Saunders. Unlike the sophisticated Franklin, Saunders was supposed to be a simple man, the "Poor Richard" ordinary readers could relate to.

SPEECH to THE
SECOND VIRGINIA CONVENTION

PATRICK HENRY

March 23, 1775

Patrick Henry was a leader in the revolutionary cause. On March 23, 1775, he made a stirring speech at the Second Virginia Convention at St. John's Church in Richmond, Virginia. Henry urged his listeners to support arming Virginia's militia to fight against England. The speech's greatness lies in its powerful statement of the ideals of liberty that make up the heart of American democracy, and for its inspiring call to action.

Subsequent generations of American schoolchildren were often required to memorize the entire speech or parts of it, especially the electrifying closing words, "give me liberty, or give me death." The following selection is from Henry's famous speech.

SPEECH TO THE SECOND VIRGINIA CONVENTION

I have but one lamp by which my feet are guided; and that is the lamp of experience. I know of no way of judging of the future but by the past. And judging by the past, I wish to know what there has been in the conduct of the British ministry for the last ten years to justify those hopes with which gentlemen have been pleased to solace themselves and the House. Is it that insidious smile with which our petition has been lately received? Trust it not, sir; it will prove a snare to your feet. Suffer not yourselves to be betrayed with a kiss. Ask yourselves how this gracious reception of our petition comports with these warlike preparations which cover our waters and darken our land. Are fleets and armies necessary to a work of love and reconciliation? Have we shown ourselves so unwilling to be reconciled, that force must be called in to win back our love? Let us not deceive ourselves, sir. These are the implements of war and subjugation; the last arguments to which kings resort. I ask gentlemen, sir, what means this martial array, if its purpose be not to force us to submission? Can gentlemen assign any other possible motives for it? Has Great Britain any enemy, in this quarter of the world, to call for all this accumulation of navies and armies? No, sir, she has none. They are meant for us; they can be meant for no other. They are sent over to bind and rivet upon us those chains which the British ministry have been so long forging. And what have we to oppose to them? Shall we try argument? Sir, we have been trying that for the last ten years. Have we anything new to offer on the subject? Nothing. We have held the subject up in every light of which it is capable; but it has been all in vain. Shall we resort to entreaty and humble supplication? What terms shall we find which have not been already exhausted? Let us not, I beseech you, sir, deceive ourselves longer. Sir, we have done everything that could be done to avert the storm which is now coming on. . . . There is no longer any room for hope. If we wish to be free—if we mean to preserve inviolate those inestimable privileges for which we have been so long contending—if we mean not basely to abandon the noble struggle in which we have been so long engaged, and which we have pledged ourselves never to abandon until the glorious object of our contest shall be obtained, we must fight! I repeat it, sir, we must fight! An appeal to arms and to the God of Hosts is all that is left us!

They tell us, sir. that we are weak; . . . Sir, we are not weak, if we make a proper use of the means which the God of nature hath placed in our power. Three millions of people, armed in the holy cause of liberty, and in such a country as that which we possess, are invincible by any force which our enemy can send against us. Besides, sir, we shall not fight our battles alone. There is a just God who presides over the destinies of nations; and who will raise friends to fight our battles for us.

The battle, sir, is not to the strong alone; it is to the vigilant, the active, the brave. Besides, sir, we have no election. If we were base enough to desire it, it is now too late to retire from the contest. There is no retreat but in submission and slavery! Our chains are forged! Their clanking may be heard on the plains of Boston! The war is inevitable—and let it come! I repeat it, sir, let it come!

It is in vain, sir, to extenuate the matter. Gentlemen may cry Peace, Peace—but there is no peace. The war is actually begun! The next gale that sweeps from the North will bring to our ears the clash of resounding arms! Our brethren are already in the field! Why stand we here idle? What is it that gentlemen wish? What would they have? Is life so dear, or peace so sweet, as to be purchased at the price of chains and slavery? Forbid it, Almighty God! I know not what course others may take; but as for me, give me liberty, or give me death!

Patrick Henry was known by contemporaries for his impassioned nature and his ability to sway listeners with strong emotions.

In 1765 the English Parliament passed the Stamp Act. The act gave the British the power to tax all printed colonial documents, including newspapers, almanacs, and legal documents. Many colonists were furious because they felt they should not be taxed without their consent. Patrick Henry spoke in the Virginia legislature against the act. His speech was interrupted by cries of "Treason! Treason!" from legislators loyal to the king. Henry immediately replied, "If this be treason, make the most of it."

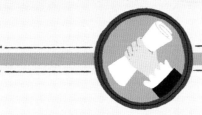

AUTHOR

Patrick Henry (1739–1799) became a member of the Virginia legislature in 1763. Born to a wealthy Virginia family, he tried farming and storekeeping before becoming a lawyer in 1760. In the legislature, he spoke out passionately against British tyranny and demanded colonial independence. Henry was also a delegate to the First Continental Congress in 1774 and the Second Continental Congress in 1775. During and after the Revolution, he served five times as Virginia's governor, and was among the leading advocates of adding a Bill of Rights to the new Constitution (which he opposed) in 1787.

RESPONSE

Henry's fiery speech helped move many colonists closer to the idea of independence from England.

Patrick Henry made his famous 1775 speech to the Second Virginia Convention while they met in a church, not in their official building. The English governor of the colony had shut down the legislature in 1769, in part responding to Henry's defiant leadership against the hated Stamp Act, but the legislators continued to meet on their own. Above, the Assembly reacts to Henry's speech.

Henry refused to attend the Constitutional Convention in Philadelphia in May 1787, saying he "smelt a rat." Later, after the new Constitution was published, he complained, "Who authorized them to speak the language of We the people?" Henry also criticized the document for not containing a bill of rights. People listened. In 1789 in Virginia, James Madison presented to Congress the amendments that became the Bill of Rights.

One observer said about Patrick Henry, "He is by far the most powerful speaker I ever heard. Every word he says not only engages, but commands the attention. . . ."

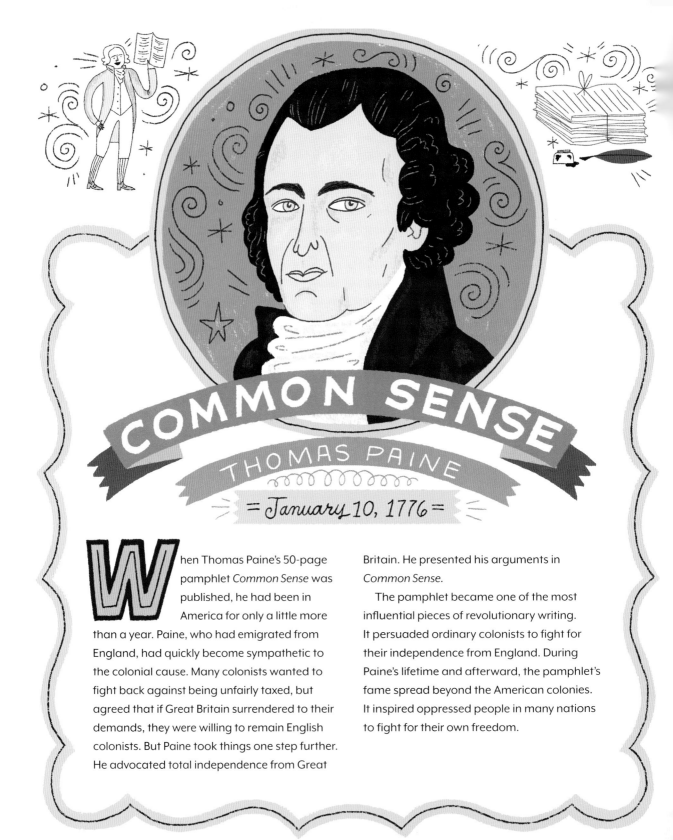

COMMON SENSE

THOMAS PAINE

= January 10, 1776 =

When Thomas Paine's 50-page pamphlet *Common Sense* was published, he had been in America for only a little more than a year. Paine, who had emigrated from England, had quickly become sympathetic to the colonial cause. Many colonists wanted to fight back against being unfairly taxed, but agreed that if Great Britain surrendered to their demands, they were willing to remain English colonists. But Paine took things one step further. He advocated total independence from Great Britain. He presented his arguments in *Common Sense.*

The pamphlet became one of the most influential pieces of revolutionary writing. It persuaded ordinary colonists to fight for their independence from England. During Paine's lifetime and afterward, the pamphlet's fame spread beyond the American colonies. It inspired oppressed people in many nations to fight for their own freedom.

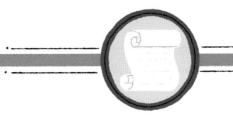

COMMON SENSE

I have heard it asserted by some, that as America hath flourished under her former connection with Great Britain, the same connection is necessary towards her future happiness, and will always have the same effect. Nothing can be more fallacious than this kind of argument. We may as well assert that because a child has thriven upon milk, that it is never to have meat, or that the first twenty years of our lives is to become a precedent for the next twenty. But even this is admitting more than is true; for I answer roundly, that America would have flourished as much, and probably much more, had no European power taken any notice of her. The commerce by which she enriched herself are the necessaries of life, and will always have a market while eating is the custom of Europe.

But she has protected us, say some. That she hath engrossed us is true, and defended the continent at our expense as well as her own is admitted. . . .

Alas! we have been long led away by ancient prejudices, and made large sacrifices to superstition. We have boasted the protection of Great Britain without considering that her motive was interest, not attachment: and that she did not protect us from our enemies on our account, but from her enemies on her own account, from those who had no quarrel with us on any other account., but who will always be our enemies on the same account. Let Britain waive her pretensions to the continent, or the continent throw off the dependence, and we should be at peace with France and Spain were they at war with Britain. . . .

But Britain is the parent country, say some. Then the more shame upon her conduct. Even brutes do not devour their young, nor savages make war upon their families; wherefore, the assertion, if true, turns to her reproach: but it happens not to be true, or only partly so, and the phrase parent or mother country hath been jesuitically adopted by the king and his parasites, with a low, papistical design of gaining an unfair bias on the credulous weakness of our minds. Europe, and not England, is the parent country of America. This new world hath been the asylum for the persecuted lovers of civil and religious liberty from every part of Europe. Hither have they fled, not from the tender embraces of a mother, but from the cruelty of the monster; and it is so far true of England, that the same tyranny which drove the first emigrants from home, pursues their descendants still. . . .

I challenge the warmest advocate for reconciliation to show a single advantage that this continent can reap, by being connected with Great Britain. I repeat the challenge, not a single advantage is derived. Our corn will fetch its price in any market in Europe, and our imported goods must be paid for, buy them where we will. . . .

Every quiet method for peace hath been ineffectual. Our prayers have been rejected with disdain: and have tended to convince us that nothing flatters vanity or confirms obstinacy in kings more than repeated petitioning—and nothing hath contributed more than that very measure to make the kings of Europe absolute [have total power]. . . . Wherefore, since nothing but blows will do, for God's sake let us come to a final separation, and not leave the next generation to be cutting throats under the violated unmeaning names of parent and child.

To say they will never attempt it [English violations of the colonists' rights and property] again is idle and visionary: we thought so as the repeal of the stamp act, yet a year or two undeceived us; as well may we suppose that nations which have been once defeated will never renew the quarrel.

As to government matters, it is not in the power of Britain to do this continent justice: the business of it will soon be too weighty and intricate to be managed with any tolerable degree of convenience, by a power so distant from us, and so very ignorant of us; for if they cannot conquer us, they cannot govern us. . . .

Small islands not capable of protecting themselves are the proper objects for kingdoms to take under their care; but there is something very absurd in supposing a continent to be perpetually governed by an island. In no instance hath nature made the satellite larger than its primary planet; and as England and America, with respect to each other, reverse the common order of nature, it is evident that they belong to different systems. England to Europe: America to itself. . . .

But where, say some, is the king of America? I'll tell you, friend, he reigns above, and doth not make havoc of mankind like the Royal Brute of Great Britain. Yet that we may not appear to be defective even in earthly honors, let a day be solemnly set apart for proclaiming the charter; let it be brought forth placed on the divine law, the Word of God; let a crown be placed thereon, by which the world may know, that so far as we approve of monarchy, that in America THE LAW IS KING. For as in absolute governments the king is law, so in free countries the law ought to be king, and there ought to be no other. But lest any ill use should afterwards arise, let the crown at the conclusion of the ceremony be demolished, and scattered among the people whose right it is.

A government of our own is our natural right; and when a man seriously reflects on the precariousness of human affairs, he will become convinced, that it is infinitely wiser and safer to form a constitution of our own in a cool deliberate manner, while we have it in our power, than to trust such an interesting event to time and chance. . . .

O ye that love mankind! Ye that dare oppose not only the tyranny but the tyrant, stand forth! Every spot of the old world is overrun with oppression. Freedom hath been hunted round the globe. Asia and Africa have long expelled her. Europe regards her like a stranger, and England hath given her warning to depart. O receive the fugitive, and prepare in time an asylum for mankind. ★

AUTHOR

Thomas Paine (1737–1809) worked as a corset maker and as a tax collector in England before immigrating to Philadelphia in 1774. There, he became a journalist. After *Common Sense,* he wrote a series of pamphlets defending the American Revolution (1775–1783). One of these pamphlets, *The Crisis,* began with the famous phrase, "These are the times that try men's souls." Paine was an early and vocal opponent of slavery, and a critic of organized religion—views that hurt his reputation in his day.

In this engraving, British troops arrive in Concord, Massachusetts, on April 19, 1775. Later, the troops met colonial Minutemen on the North Bridge. The battle that followed began the Revolutionary War.

RESPONSE

Only three months after its publication in January 1776, 120,000 copies of *Common Sense* had been sold. The American population then numbered 2.5 million. One of every 20 people had a copy. Almost every colonist read this bestseller or heard it discussed. It remains widely read today.

The two-line poem on the bottom of the title page of Thomas Paine's *Common Sense* reads "Man knows no Master save creating Heaven,/Or those whom choice and common good ordain." The poem suggests that the American colonies should be ruled by only God or rulers they freely choose and who iron out what is best for most people. Here Paine is clearly saying that the colonists should not accept English rule because the common good of the colonies is of no interest to Great Britain.

Paine stopped going to school at the age of thirteen, when he became an apprentice in his father's corset shop in England. In 1757, after an unsuccessful attempt to run away to sea, he opened his own shop.

In 1774 Paine met Benjamin Franklin in London. That year Franklin sent him to the American colonies with letters introducing Paine to Franklin's friends in Philadelphia.

Although Paine was a recent immigrant, he felt at home in colonial America and even served in the revolutionary army. Said Paine, "Where liberty is, there is my country."

LETTER to JOHN ADAMS

ABIGAIL ADAMS

March 31, 1776

n March 1776 John Adams was in Philadelphia attending the Continental Congress. He left his wife, Abigail, and children behind at their Massachusetts farm. In this letter, Abigail gently but firmly reminds her husband that women should also have rights in the new nation, including the right to vote. When she wrote that women should vote, Abigail Adams was 154 years ahead of her time. American women gained this right in 1920, with the ratification of the Nineteenth Amendment.

LETTER TO JOHN ADAMS

. . . I long to hear that you have declared an independency—and by the way in the new Code of Laws which I suppose it will be necessary for you to make I desire you would Remember the Ladies, and be more generous and favourable to them than your ancestors. Do not put such unlimited power into the hands of the Husbands. Remember all Men would be tyrants if they could. If particular care and attention is not paid to the Ladies we are determined to foment a Rebellion, and will not hold ourselves bound by any Laws in which we have no voice, or Representation.

That your Sex are Naturally Tyrannical is a Truth so thoroughly established as to admit of no dispute, but such of you as wish to be happy willingly give up the harsh title of Master for the more tender and endearing one of Friend. Why then, not put it out of the power of the vicious and the Lawless to use us with cruelty and indignity with impunity. Men of Sense in all Ages abhor those customs which treat us only as the vassals [servants] of your Sex. Regard us then as Beings placed by providence under your protection and in imitation of the Supreme Being make use of that power only for our happiness.★

An engraving shows women voting in New Jersey at the end of the eighteenth century. New Jersey's 1776 constitution granted the vote to anyone who possessed a certain amount of money. This phrasing accidentally permitted white widows and unmarried women who owned property to vote. But in 1807 the state legislature took away this right from women property owners.

Abigail Adams spoke frequently to her husband John about women's rights. In another letter, she said that men continued to insist on maintaining complete power over their wives. She then warned her husband, "But you must remember, that arbitrary power is like most other things which are very hard, very liable to be broken."

AUTHOR

Abigail Adams (1744–1818) was the wife of John Adams, who became the second president of the United States. Born in Massachusetts, she educated herself to a degree far beyond that of most colonial women. In 1764, at the age of nineteen, she married John Adams. Revolutionary politics required that her husband travel widely, often without her. While he was away, she took care of the farm and the household, bought land, and dealt with tenants. Their eldest son, John Quincy Adams, became the sixth president in 1824.

RESPONSE

Several months after Abigail composed the letter, Adams wrote to a lawyer named James Sullivan and declared that it was impossible for everyone to have the right to vote. He also said that women were unfit for political life but fit for caring for home and children.

This engraving of Abigail Adams late in life captures her frank gaze and the force of her character. Adams believed that "If we mean to have heroes, statesmen and philosophers, We should have learned women."

Abigail Adams had a gift for writing. But it was almost impossible for colonial women to publish anything. She, like many of her female contemporaries, expressed herself in letters.

DECLARATION of INDEPENDENCE

PASSED ON July 2, 1776; RATIFIED ON July 4, 1776

On June 11, 1776, the Second Continental Congress appointed a committee to draft a declaration of independence from England. The committee included Thomas Jefferson, Benjamin Franklin, and John Adams. Jefferson was asked by the committee to write the document. His draft attempted to justify American independence from England by listing the wrongs the mother country had inflicted on the colonists. Jefferson also sketched a basic philosophy of democratic government, asserting that the rights of citizens flow from the laws of nature and of God—and that governments, in turn, gain their power from the consent of the governed.

On June 28, the committee submitted Jefferson's draft to the Congress. The delegates debated and amended the declaration before passing it on July 2 and ratifying it on July 4. Ironically, Jefferson, who was a slaveholder, had initially drafted a section condemning the English king for engaging in the slave trade—"a cruel war against human nature itself"—but opposition from Southern leaders and New England mercantile interests caused Congress to cut it. Those who signed the document knew that they were committing treason against England and might possibly be executed for their crime. Nevertheless, every delegate to the Continental Congress signed the declaration.

The Declaration of Independence is considered to be one of the greatest expressions of the nature of human freedom. The central section of the declaration is a ringing assertion that every human being has an equal right to life, liberty, and the pursuit of happiness.

THE UNANIMOUS DECLARATION
OF THE THIRTEEN UNITED STATES OF AMERICA

When in the Course of human events, it becomes necessary for one people to dissolve the political bands which have connected them with another, and to assume among the Powers of the earth, the separate and equal station to which the Laws of Nature and of Nature's God entitle them, a decent respect to the opinions of mankind requires that they should declare the causes which impel them to the separation. —We hold these truths to be self-evident, that all men are created equal, that they are endowed by their Creator with certain unalienable Rights, that among these are Life, Liberty and the Pursuit of Happiness. —That to secure these rights, Governments are instituted among Men, deriving their just powers from the consent of the governed, —That whenever any Form of Government becomes destructive of these ends, it is the Right of the People to alter or to abolish it, and to institute new Government, laying its foundation on such principles and organizing its powers in such form, as to them shall seem most likely to effect their Safety and Happiness. Prudence, indeed, will dictate that Governments long established should not be changed for light and transient causes: and accordingly all experience hath shewn, that mankind are more disposed to suffer, while evils are sufferable, than to right themselves by abolishing the forms to which they are accustomed. But when a long train of abuses and usurpations, pursuing invariably the same Object evinces a design to reduce them under absolute Despotism, it is their right, it is their duty, to throw off such Government, and to provide new Guards for their future security. —Such has been the patient sufferance of these Colonies: and such is now the necessity which constrains them to alter their former Systems of Government. The history of the present King of Great Britain is a history of repeated injuries and usurpations, all having in direct object the establishment of an absolute Tyranny over these States. To prove this, let Facts be submitted to a candid world. —He has refused his Assent to Laws, the most wholesome and necessary for the public good. —He has forbidden his Governors to pass Laws of immediate and pressing importance, unless suspended in their operation till his Assent should be obtained; and when so suspended, he has utterly neglected to attend to them. —He has refused to pass other Laws for the accommodation of large districts of people, unless those people would relinquish the right of Representation in the Legislature, a right inestimable to them and formidable to tyrants only. —He has called together legislative bodies at places unusual, uncomfortable, and distant from the depository' of their public Records, for the sole purpose of fatiguing them into compliance with his measures. —He has dissolved Representative Houses repeatedly, for opposing with manly firmness his invasions on the rights of the people. —He has refused for a long time, after such dissolutions, to cause others to be elected; whereby the Legislative powers, incapable of Annihilation, have returned to the People at large for their exercise; the State remaining in the mean time exposed to all the dangers of invasion from without, and convulsions within. —He has endeavoured to prevent the population of these States; for that purpose obstructing the Laws for Naturalization of Foreigners; refusing to pass others to encourage their migrations hither, and raising the conditions of new Appropriations of Lands. —He has obstructed the Administration of Justice, by refusing his Assent to Laws for establishing Judiciary powers. —He has made Judges dependent on his Will alone, for the tenure of their' offices, and the amount and payment of their salaries. —He has erected a multitude of New Offices, and sent hither swarms of Officers to harass our people, and eat out their substance. —He has kept among us, in times of peace, Standing Armies without the Consent of our legislatures. —He has affected to render the Military independent of and superior to the Civil power. —He has combined with others to subject us to a jurisdiction foreign to our constitution, and unacknowledged by our laws; giving his Assent to their Acts of pretended Legislation: —For quartering large bodies of armed troops among us: —For protecting them, by a mock Trial, "from punishment for any Murders which they should commit on the Inhabitants of these States: —For cutting off our Trade with all parts of the world: —For imposing Taxes on us without our Consent: —For depriving us in many cases, of the benefits of Trial by Jury: —For transporting us beyond Seas to be tried for pretended offences: —For abolishing the free System of English Laws in a neighboring Province, establishing therein an Arbitrary government, and enlarging its Boundaries so as to render it at once an example and fit instrument for introducing (he same absolute rule into these Colonies: —For taking away our Charters, abolishing our most valuable Laws, and altering fundamentally the Forms of our Governments: —For suspending our own Legislatures, and declaring themselves invested with power to legislate for us in all cases whatsoever. —He has abdicated Government here, by declaring us out of his Protection and waging War against us. —He has plundered our seas, ravaged our Coasts, burnt our towns, and destroyed the Lives of our people. —He is at this time transporting large Armies of foreign Mercenaries to complete the works of death, desolation and tyranny, already begun with circumstances of Cruelty & perfidy scarcely paralleled in the most barbarous ages, and totally unworthy the Head of a civilized nation. —He has constrained our fellow Citizens taken Captive on the high Seas to bear Arms against their Country, to become the executioners of their friends and Brethren, or to fall themselves by their Hands. —He has excited domestic insurrections amongst us, and has endeavoured to bring on the inhabitants of our frontiers, the merciless Indian Savages, whose known rule of warfare, is an undistinguished destruction of all ages, sexes, and conditions. In every stage of these Oppressions We have Petitioned for Redress in the most humble terms: Our repeated Petitions have been answered only by repeated injury. A Prince, whose character is thus marked by every act which may define a Tyrant, is unfit to be the ruler of a free people. Nor have We been wanting in attentions to our British brethren. We have warned them from time to time of attempts by their legislature to extend an unwarrantable jurisdiction over us. We have reminded them of the circumstances of our emigration and settlement here. We have appealed to their native justice and magnanimity, and we have conjured them by the ties of our common kindred to disavow these usurpations, which, would inevitably interrupt our connections and correspondence. They too have been deaf to the voice of justice and of consanguinity. We must, therefore, acquiesce in the necessity, which denounces our Separation, and hold them, as we hold the result of mankind, Enemies in War, in Peace Friends. —

We therefore, the Representatives of the United States of America, in General Congress, Assembled, appealing to the Supreme Judge of the world for the rectitude of our intentions, do, in the Name, and by Authority of the good People of these Colonies, solemnly publish and declare, That these United Colonies are, and of Right ought to be Free and Independent States; that they are Absolved from all Allegiance to the British Crown, and that all political connection between them and the State of Great Britain, is and ought to be totally dissolved; and that as Free and Independent States, they have full Power to levy War, conclude Peace, contract Alliances, establish Commerce, and to do all other Acts and Things which Independent States may of right do. —And for the support of this Declaration, with a firm reliance on the protection of divine Providence, we mutually pledge to each other our Lives, our Fortunes and our sacred Honor. ★

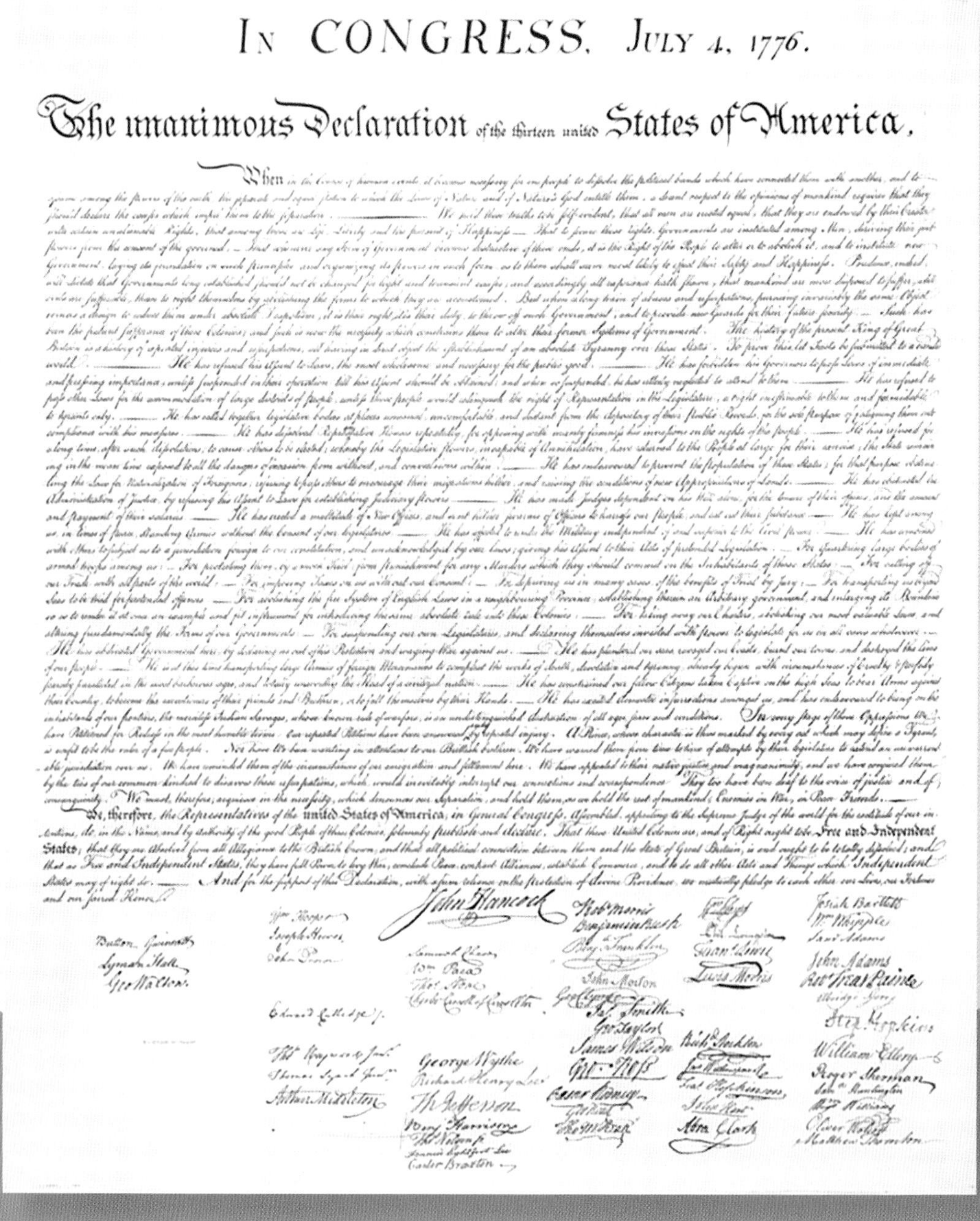
IN CONGRESS, JULY 4, 1776.

The unanimous Declaration of the thirteen united States of America,

The Declaration of Independence was first printed on July 4–5, 1776, by John Dunlap of Philadelphia, a printer to the Continental Congress.

AUTHOR

Thomas Jefferson (1743–1826) was a young Virginia planter and lawyer when he wrote the Declaration of Independence. But he already had the reputation of being a skilled writer. The democratic ideals Jefferson included were popular among liberal thinkers of his time. But they had never been used by a people to justify their right to rise up against their ruler and establish their own independent government. Jefferson believed that slavery was morally wrong, but nonetheless owned slaves throughout his lifetime and feared a race war if American slaves were freed. In 1801 Jefferson became the third president of the United States.

RESPONSE

France recognized the new nation in 1778. But the rest of Europe did not, fearing British anger. And of course England itself refused to recognize American independence until it lost the Revolutionary War in 1781. In the 1783 Treaty of Paris, which formally ended the war, Great Britain acknowledged the United States to be "free, sovereign, and independent."

The Declaration of Independence was approved by Congress on July 4, 1776, but the men who signed it on that day, Charles Thomson and John Hancock, signed only a draft. The official parchment copy was not signed by the delegates until August 2.

Thomas Jefferson at first doubted that he was skillful enough to draft the declaration, but other delegates he respected convinced him that he was the right person for the job.

Jefferson wrote the draft on a portable writing desk that he pulled onto his lap at his lodgings on the outskirts of Philadelphia.

The Continental Congress never called the document the Declaration of Independence.

FEDERALIST Nº 78

ALEXANDER HAMILTON

May 28, 1788

By 1787, most Americans agreed that the decentralized system of government under the Articles of Confederation (see p. 39) was too chaotic. Each state was like a mini-country. Every state printed its own paper money, made and interpreted its own laws, had its own militia, set its own tax and export policy.

The members of Congress called for a Constitutional Convention. After lengthy and impassioned debate, the document that became our current Constitution was passed. But now it had to be ratified by the states, and the states were not eager to cede power to a new federal government.

So James Madison, John Jay, and Alexander Hamilton went to work publishing eighty-five essays in support of the Constitution, known today collectively as the Federalist Papers. In the one excerpted here, Hamilton argues for the importance of an independent judiciary. He says that only judges appointed for life ("during good behavior") would guarantee that they would be insulated from political and financial pressure and render independent and just decisions. It is one of the Federalist Papers most often cited today.

FEDERALIST NO. 78

To the People of the State of New-York.

WE proceed now to an examination of the judiciary department of the proposed government.

In unfolding the defects of the existing confederation, the utility and necessity of a federal judicature have been clearly pointed out. . . .

According to the plan of the convention, all the judges who may be appointed by the United States are to hold their offices during good behaviour, which is conformable to the most approved of the state constitutions; and among the rest, to that of this state. Its propriety having been drawn into question by the adversaries of that plan, is no light symptom of the rage for objection which disorders their imaginations and judgments. The standard of good behaviour for the continuance in office of the judicial magistracy is certainly one of the most valuable of the modern improvements in the practice of government. In a monarchy it is an excellent barrier to the despotism of the prince: In a republic it is a no less excellent barrier to the encroachments and oppressions of the representative body. And it is the best expedient which can be devised in any government, to secure a steady, upright and impartial administration of the laws.

Whoever attentively considers the different departments of power must perceive, that in a government in which they are separated from each other, the judiciary, from the nature of its functions, will always be the least dangerous to the political rights of the constitution; because it will be least in a capacity to annoy or injure them. The executive not only dispenses the honors, but holds the sword of the community. The legislature not only commands the purse, but prescribes the rules by which the duties and rights of every citizen are to be regulated. The judiciary on the contrary has no influence over either the sword or the purse, no direction either of the strength or of the wealth of the society, and can take no active resolution whatever. It may truly be said to have neither force nor will, but merely judgment; and must ultimately depend upon the aid of the executive arm even for the efficacy of its judgments.

This simple view of the matter suggests several important consequences. It proves incontestibly that the judiciary is beyond comparison the weakest of the three departments of power; that it can never attack with success either of the other two; and that all possible care is requisite to enable it to defend itself against their attacks. It equally proves, that though individual oppression may now and then proceed from the courts of justice, the general liberty of the people can never be

→

endangered from that quarter; I mean, so long as the judiciary remains truly distinct from both the legislative and executive. For I agree that "there is no liberty, if the power of judging be not separated from the legislative and executive powers." And it proves, in the last place, that as liberty can have nothing to fear from the judiciary alone, but would have every thing to fear from its union with either of the other departments; that as all the effects of such an union must ensue from a dependence of the former on the latter, notwithstanding a nominal and apparent separation; that as from the natural feebleness of the judiciary, it is in continual jeopardy of being overpowered, awed or influenced by its coordinate branches; and that as nothing can contribute so much to its firmness and independence, as permanency in office, this quality may therefore be justly regarded as an indispensable ingredient in its constitution; and in a great measure as the citadel of the public justice and the public security.

The complete independence of the courts of justice is peculiarly essential in a limited constitution. By a limited constitution I understand one which contains certain specified exceptions to the legislative authority; such for instance as that it shall pass no bills of attainder, no ex post facto laws, and the like. Limitations of this kind can be preserved in practice no other way than through the medium of the courts of justice; whose duty it must be to declare all acts contrary to the manifest tenor of the constitution void. Without this, all the reservations of particular rights or privileges would amount to nothing.

. . . No legislative act therefore contrary to the constitution can be valid. To deny this would be to affirm that the deputy is greater than his principal; that the servant is above his master; that the representatives of the people are superior to the people themselves; that men acting by virtue of powers may do not only what their powers do not authorise, but what they forbid.

. . . The interpretation of the laws is the proper and peculiar province of the courts. A constitution is in fact, and must be, regarded by the judges as a fundamental law. It therefore belongs to them to ascertain its meaning as well as the meaning of any particular act proceeding from the legislative body. If there should happen to be an irreconcileable variance between the two, that which has the superior obligation and validity ought of course to be preferred; or in other words, the constitution ought to be preferred to the statute, the intention of the people to the intention of their agents.

Nor does this conclusion by any means suppose a superiority of the judicial to the legislative power. It only supposes that the power of the people is superior to both; and that where the will of the legislature declared in its statutes, stands in opposition to that of the people declared in the constitution, the judges ought to be governed by the latter, rather than the former. They ought to regulate their decisions by the fundamental laws, rather than by those which are not fundamental.

. . . If then the courts of justice are to be considered as the bulwarks of a limited constitution against legislative encroachments, this consideration will afford a strong argument for the permanent tenure of judicial offices, since nothing will contribute so much as this to that independent spirit in the judges, which must be essential to the faithful performance of so arduous a duty.

This independence of the judges is equally requisite to guard the constitution and the rights of individuals from the effects of those ill humours which the arts of designing men, or the influence of particular conjunctures, sometimes disseminate among the people themselves, and which, though they speedily give place to better information and more deliberate reflection, have a tendency in the mean time to occasion dangerous innovations in the government, and serious oppressions of the minor party in the community.

. . . But it is not with a view to infractions of the constitution only that the independence of the judges may be an essential safeguard against the effects of occasional ill humours in the society. These sometimes extend no farther than to the injury of the private rights of particular classes of citizens, by unjust and partial laws. Here also the firmness of the judicial magistracy is of vast importance in mitigating the severity, and confining the operation of such laws. It not only serves to moderate the immediate mischiefs of those which may have been passed, but it operates as a check upon the legislative body in passing them; who, perceiving that obstacles to the success of an iniquitous intention are to be expected from the scruples of the courts, are in a manner compelled by the very motives of the injustice they meditate, to qualify their attempts. This is a circumstance calculated to have more influence upon the character of our governments, than but few may be aware of.

. . . That inflexible and uniform adherence to the rights of the constitution and of individuals, which we perceive to be indispensable in the courts of justice, can certainly not be expected from judges who hold their offices by a temporary commission. Periodical appointments, however regulated, or by whomsoever made, would in some way or other be fatal to their necessary independence. If the power of making them was committed either to the executive or legislature, there would be danger of an improper complaisance to the branch which possessed it; if to both, there would be an unwillingness to hazard the displeasure of either; if to the people, or to persons chosen by them for the special purpose, there would be too great a disposition to consult popularity, to justify a reliance that nothing would be consulted but the constitution and the laws.

. . . Upon the whole there can be no room to doubt that the convention acted wisely in copying from the models of those constitutions which have established good behaviour as the tenure of their judicial offices in point of duration; and that so far from being blameable on this account, their plan would have been inexcuseably defective if it had wanted this important feature of good government. . . .

PUBLIUS. ★

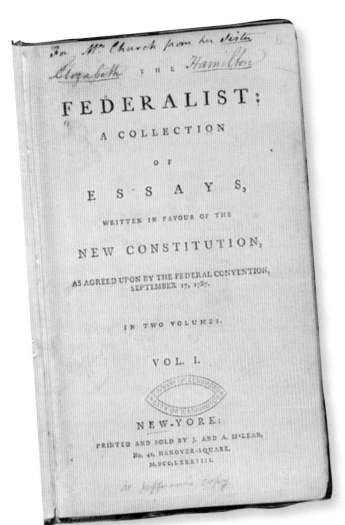

THE Hamilton

FEDERALIST:

A COLLECTION

OF

ESSAYS,

WRITTEN IN FAVOUR OF THE

NEW CONSTITUTION,

AS AGREED UPON BY THE FEDERAL CONVENTION,
SEPTEMBER 17, 1787.

IN TWO VOLUMES.

VOL. I.

NEW-YORK:

PRINTED AND SOLD BY J. AND A. M'LEAN,
No. 41, HANOVER-SQUARE.
M.DCC.LXXXVIII.

One state in which the battle over ratifying the Constitution raged fiercely was New York. Alexander Hamilton and John Jay, both New York lawyers and politicians, joined with James Madison in writing eighty-five articles in order to persuade voters to approve the new system of government. They sent these as letters to newspapers, which published them in 1787–1788. These articles are called the *Federalist Papers.*

The Federalist Papers were published first in newspapers in Hamilton's home city of New York, but word quickly spread and newspapers in other states reprinted them. The essays were published in book form in 1788, with revisions and corrections by Hamilton. Another edition, published in 1818, with revisions and corrections by Madison, was the first to identify each essay by its author's name. Because of this publishing history, the exact wording varies slightly in different editions of The Federalist, and there is conflicting information as to who wrote several of the essays.

Hamilton not only wrote the majority of the Federalist Papers, he outlined all of the subjects to be covered and enlisted the aid of John Jay and James Madison to write the others. The authorship of a few of the Federalist essays is uncertain, but it is believed that Jay, who became the nation's first chief justice, wrote 5; Madison, the fourth president, wrote 29; the prolific Alexander Hamilton wrote 51.

Madison, Hamilton, and Jay signed their articles with the pen name "Publius," for one of the founders and heroes of the Roman republic.

AUTHOR

Born on the Caribbean island of Nevis in 1755, Alexander Hamilton was orphaned at age thirteen. Left to fend for himself, Hamilton found work with a shipping company before leaving for North America in 1772 with the help of a local minister. By 1774, he had immersed himself in the growing rebellion against British rule and had assumed a leadership role. He served as George Washington's chief aide during the Revolutionary War, and later as the nation's first Treasury Secretary under Washington—a job that saw him almost singlehandedly build the foundation of America's present-day financial system. Hamilton's political fortunes declined after Washington's death in 1799, and he turned to his already flourishing private law practice. In 1800, he successfully defended a young man accused of murder in a high-profile case, working together with his co-counsel, another well-known attorney and politician named Aaron Burr. Four years later Burr, who was the sitting vice president of the United States at the time, killed Hamilton in a duel. Hamilton was a great believer in the importance of a strong central government for the United States, and was one of the Constitution's most effective advocates.

RESPONSE

The Constitution was ratified in 1789. The Federalist essays were widely read and discussed, but historians disagree about how much of a factor they were in the Constitution's ratification. It was not Hamilton's intention, but the Federalist essays are almost certainly more influential today than they were in his time. Federalist No. 78 is among the most frequently cited documents by the United States Supreme Court. True to Hamilton's reasoning, federal courts have served as an effective check on Congress and on the president—look no further than the Supreme Court rulings in this book to see powerful examples of this.

After the Revolutionary War, the newly independent American states were bound together by a loose agreement called the Articles of Confederation. There was no executive branch (no president), and no judiciary branch. The federal government had no power to levy taxes, and could not afford a standing army. The framers of the Articles, having just rid themselves of the British monarchy, were afraid of too much centralized power. So they called for only one branch of a central government—a Congress elected by the people, whose main role was to conduct foreign policy and provide for the common defense. The new Constitution would address those weaknesses.

THE CONSTITUTION

PASSED BY CONGRESS *September 17, 1787*; RATIFIED *June 21, 1788*

THE BILL OF RIGHTS

PASSED BY CONGRESS *September 25, 1789*; RATIFIED *December 15, 1791*

On May 25, 1787, 55 delegates from 12 states (every state except Rhode Island) met at the State House in Philadelphia to revise the Articles of Confederation. The need for revision was urgent because the government had no power to regulate commerce, levy taxes, or act for the common defense of all the states. Soon, however, the delegates decided to write a new constitution. This version focused on establishing a strong national government and a "checks and balances" system among the three branches of government (legislative, executive, and judiciary). Unsurprisingly, there were many objections. Some delegates argued that individual rights were being neglected. Others, that small states would suffer at the hands of the large. That's why tiny Rhode Island boycotted the convention altogether, the only state not to send a delegate.

In order to gain support for the Constitution from those concerned about individual rights being trampled by an overly strong central government, James Madison promised to add amendments after ratification. He presented a drafted set of amendments to the House of Representatives on June 8, 1789, claiming they would protect "the great rights of mankind." After both houses of Congress passed 12 of the amendments, the states ratified 10 of them and the Bill of Rights was added to the Constitution in 1791.

The U.S. Constitution is the oldest written national constitution in the world. Once it was ratified, the experience of the new nation soon proved its utility and soundness as a blueprint

for a new kind of government, and it has been long lauded as the "supreme law of the land."

The Bill of Rights is admired throughout the world as one of the simplest and most effective documents protecting individual liberties. It defined and secured the individual rights of Americans without weakening the Constitution. Although the Constitution has been amended twenty-seven times—most recently in 1992—the Bill of Rights has remained untouched.

THE CONSTITUTION

WE THE PEOPLE of the United States, in order to form a more perfect Union, establish Justice, insure domestic Tranquility, provide for the common defence, promote the general Welfare, and secure the Blessings of Liberty to ourselves and our Posterity, do ordain and establish this Constitution for the United States of America.

ARTICLE I.

Section 1. All legislative Powers herein granted shall be vested in a Congress of the United States, which shall consist of a Senate and House of Representatives.

Section 2. The House of Representatives shall be composed of Members chosen every second Year by the People of the several States, and the Electors in each State shall have the Qualifications requisite for Electors of the most numerous Branch of the State Legislature.

No Person shall be a Representative who shall not have attained to the Age of twenty-five Years, and been seven Years a Citizen of the United States, and who shall not, when elected, be an Inhabitant of that State in which he shall be chosen.

Representatives and direct Taxes shall be apportioned among the several States which may be included within this Union, according to their respective Numbers, which shall be determined by adding to the whole Number of free Persons, including those bound to Service for a Term of Years, and excluding Indians not taxed, three-fifths of all other

Persons [Modified by Amendment XIV]. The actual Enumeration shall be made within three Years after the first Meeting of the Congress of the United States, and within every subsequent Term of ten Years, in such Manner as they shall by Law direct. The Number of Representatives shall not exceed one for every thirty Thousand, but each State shall have at Least one Representative; and until such enumeration shall be made, the State of New Hampshire shall be entitled to choose three, Massachusetts eight, Rhode-Island and Providence Plantations one, Connecticut five, New-York six, New Jersey four, Pennsylvania eight, Delaware one, Maryland six, Virginia ten, North Carolina five, South Carolina five, and Georgia three.

When vacancies happen in the Representation from any State, the Executive Authority thereof shall issue Writs of Election to fill such Vacancies. The House of Representatives shall choose their Speaker and other Officers; and shall have the sole Power of Impeachment.

Section 3. The Senate of the United States shall be composed of two Senators from each State, chosen by the Legislature thereof [Modified by Amendment XVII], for six Years; and each Senator shall have one Vote.

Immediately after they shall be assembled in Consequence of the first Election, they shall be divided as equally as may be into three Classes. The Seats of the Senators of the first Class shall be vacated at the Expiration of the second Year, of the second Class at the Expiration of the fourth Year, and of the third Class at the Expiration of the sixth Year, so that one-third may be chosen every second Year; and if Vacancies happen by Resignation, or otherwise, during the Recess of the Legislature of any State, the Executive thereof may make temporary Appointments until the next Meeting of the Legislature, which shall then fill such Vacancies [Modified by Amendment XVII].

No Person shall be a Senator who shall not have attained to the Age of thirty Years, and been nine Years a Citizen of the United States, and who shall not, when elected, be an Inhabitant of that State for which he shall be chosen.

The Vice President of the United States shall be President of the Senate, but shall have no Vote, unless they be equally divided.

The Senate shall choose their other Officers, and also a President pro tempore, in the Absence of the Vice President, or when he shall exercise the Office of President of the United States.

The Senate shall have the sole Power to try all Impeachments. When sitting for that Purpose, they shall be on Oath or Affirmation. When the President of the United States is tried, the Chief

Justice shall preside: And no Person shall be convicted without the Concurrence of two thirds of the Members present.

Judgment in Cases of Impeachment shall not extend further than to removal from Office, and disqualification to hold and enjoy any Office of honor, Trust or Profit under the United States: but the Party convicted shall nevertheless be liable and subject to Indictment, Trial. Judgment and Punishment, according to Law.

Section 4. The Times, Places and Manner of holding Elections for Senators and Representatives, shall be prescribed in each State by the Legislature thereof; but the Congress may at any time by Law make or alter such Regulations, except as to the Places of choosing Senators.

The Congress shall assemble at least once in every Year, and such Meeting shall be on the first Monday in December [Modified by Amendment XX], unless they shall by Law appoint a different Day.

Section 5. Each House shall be the Judge of the Elections, Returns and Qualifications of its own Members, and a Majority of each shall constitute a Quorum to do Business; but a smaller Number may adjourn from day to day, and may be authorized to compel the Attendance of absent Members, in such Manner, and under such Penalties as each House may provide.

Each House may determine the Rules of its Proceedings, punish its Members for disorderly Behavior, and, with the Concurrence of two-thirds, expel a Member.

Each House shall keep a Journal of its Proceedings, and from time to time publish the same, excepting such Parts as may in their Judgment require Secrecy; and the Yeas and the Nays of the Members of either House on any question shall, at the Desire of one-fifth of those Present, be entered on the Journal.

Neither House, during the Session of Congress, shall, without the Consent of the other, adjourn for more than three days, nor to any other Place than that in which the two Houses shall be sitting.

Section 6. The Senators and Representatives shall receive a Compensation for their Services, to be ascertained by Law, and paid out of the Treasury of the United States. They shall in all Cases, except Treason, Felony and Breach of the Peace, be privileged from Arrest during their Attendance at the Session of their respective Houses, and in going to and returning from the same: and for any Speech or Debate in either House, they shall not be questioned in any other Place.

No Senator or Representative shall, during the Time for which he was elected, be appointed to any civil Office under the Authority of the United States, which shall have been created, or the Emoluments [compensation] whereof shall have been increased during such time; and no

Person holding any Office under the United States, shall be a Member of either House during his Continuance in Office.

Section 7. All Bills for raising Revenue shall originate in the House of Representatives; but the Senate may propose or concur with Amendments as on other Bills.

Every Bill which shall have passed the House of Representatives and the Senate, shall, before it becomes a Law, be presented to the President of the United States; if he approve he shall sign it, but if not he shall return it, with his Objections to that House in which it shall have originated, who shall enter the Objections at large on their Journal, and proceed to reconsider it. If after such Reconsideration two thirds of that House shall agree to pass the Bill, it shall be sent, together with the Objections, to the other House, by which it shall likewise be reconsidered, and if approved by two thirds of that House, it shall become a Law. But in all such Cases the Votes of both Houses shall be determined by yeas and Nays, and the Names of the Persons voting for and against the Bill shall be entered on the Journal of each House respectively. If any Bill shall not be returned by the President within ten Days (Sundays excepted) after it shall have been presented to him, the Same shall be a Law, in like Manner as if he had signed it, unless the Congress by their Adjournment prevent its Return, in which Case it shall not be a Law.

Every Order, Resolution, or Vote to which the Concurrence of the Senate and House of Representatives may be necessary (except on a question of Adjournment) shall be presented to the President of the United States; and before the Same shall take Effect, shall be approved by him, or being disapproved by him, shall be repassed by two thirds of the Senate and House of Representatives, according to the Rules and Limitations prescribed in the Case of a Bill.

Section 8. The Congress shall have Power To lay and collect Taxes, Duties, Imposts and Excises, to pay the Debts and provide for the common Defence and general Welfare of the United States; but all Duties, Imposts and Excises shall be uniform throughout the United States;

To borrow Money on the credit of the United States;

To regulate Commerce with foreign Nations, and among the several States, and with the Indian Tribes;

To establish an uniform Rule of Naturalization, and uniform Laws on the subject of Bankruptcies through out the United States;

To coin Money, regulate the Value thereof, and of foreign Coin, and fix the Standard of Weights and Measures;

"To provide for the Punishment of counterfeiting the Securities and current Coin of the United States;

To establish Post Offices and post Roads;

To promote the Progress of Science and useful Arts, by securing for limited Times to Authors and Inventors the exclusive Right to their respective Writings and Discoveries;

To constitute Tribunals inferior to the supreme Court;

To define and punish Piracies and Felonies committed on the high Seas, and Offenses against the Law of Nations;

To declare War, grant Letters of Marque and Reprisal, and make Rules concerning Captures on Land and Water;

To raise and support Armies, but no Appropriation of Money to that Use shall be for a longer Term than two Years;

To provide and maintain a Navy;

To make Rules for the Government and Regulation of the land and naval Forces;

To provide for calling forth the Militia to execute the Laws of the Union, suppress Insurrections and repel Invasions;

To provide for organizing, arming, and disciplining the Militia, and for governing such Part of them as may be employed in the Service of the United States, reserving to the States respectively, the Appointment of the Officers, and the Authority of training the Militia according to the discipline prescribed by Congress;

To exercise exclusive Legislation in all Cases whatsoever, over such District (not exceeding ten Miles square) as may, by Cession of particular States, and the Acceptance of Congress, become the Seat of the Government of the United States, and to exercise like Authority over all Places purchased by the Consent of the Legislature of the State in which the Same shall be, for the Erection of Forts, Magazines, Arsenals, dock-Yards, and other needful Buildings;—And

To make all Laws which shall be necessary and proper for earning into Execution the foregoing Powers, and all other Powers vested by this Constitution in the Government of the United States, or in any Department or Officer thereof.

Section 9. The Migration or Importation of such Persons as any of the States now existing shall think proper to admit, shall not be prohibited by the Congress prior to the Year one thousand eight hundred and eight, but a Tax or duty may be imposed on such Importation, not exceeding ten dollars for each Person.

The Privilege of the Writ of Habeas Corpus shall not be suspended, unless when in Cases of Rebellion or Invasion the public Safety may require it.

No Bill of Attainder or ex post facto Law shall be passed.

No Capitation, or other direct, Tax shall be laid, unless in Proportion to the Census or Enumeration herein before directed to be taken.

No Tax or Duty shall be laid on Articles exported from any State.

No Preference shall be given by any Regulation of Commerce or Revenue to the Ports of one State over those of another: nor shall Vessels bound to, or from, one State, be obliged to enter, clear, or pay Duties in another.

No Money shall be drawn from the Treasury, but in Consequence of Appropriations made by Law; and a regular Statement and Account of the Receipts and Expenditures of all public Money shall be published from time to time.

No Title of Nobility shall be granted by the United States: And no Person holding any Office of Profit or Trust under them, shall, without the Consent of the Congress, accept of any present, Emolument, Office, or Title, of any kind whatever, from any King, Prince, or foreign State.

Section 10. No State shall enter into any Treaty, Alliance, or Confederation; grant Letters of Marque and Reprisal; coin Money; emit Bills of Credit; make any Thing but gold and silver Coin a Tender in Payment of Debts; pass any Bill of Attainder, ex post facto Law, or Law impairing the Obligation of Contracts, or grant any Title of Nobility.

No State shall, without the Consent of the Congress, lay any Imposts or Duties on Imports or Exports, except what may be absolutely necessary for executing its inspection Laws: and the net Produce of all Duties and Imposts, laid by any State on Imports or Exports, shall be for the Use of the Treasury of the United States; and all such Laws shall be subject to the Revision and Control of the Congress.

No State shall, without the Consent of Congress, lay any Duty of Tonnage, keep Troops, or Ships of War in time of Peace, enter into any Agreement or Compact with another State, or with a foreign Power, or engage in War, unless actually invaded, or in such imminent Danger as will not admit of delay.

ARTICLE II.

Section 1. The executive Power shall be vested in a President of the United States of America. He shall hold his Office during the Term of four Years, and, together with the Vice President, chosen for the same Term, be elected, as follows:

Each State, shall appoint, in such Manner as the Legislature, thereof may direct, a Number of Electors, equal to the whole Number of Senators and Representatives to which the State may be entitled in the Congress; but no Senator or Representative, or Person holding an Office of Trust or Profit under the United States, shall be appointed an Elector.

The Electors shall meet in their respective States, and vote by Ballot for two Persons, of whom one at least shall not be an Inhabitant of the same State with themselves. And they shall make a List of all the Persons voted for, and of the Number of Votes for each; which List they shall sign and certify, and transmit sealed to the Seat of the Government of the United States, directed to the President of the Senate. The President of the Senate shall, in the Presence of the Senate and House of Representatives, open all the Certificates, and the Votes shall then be counted. The Person having the greatest Number of Votes shall be the President, if such Number be a Majority of the whole Number of Electors appointed; and if there be more than one who have such Majority, and have an equal Number of Votes, then the House of Representatives shall immediately choose by Ballot one of them for President; and if no Person have a Majority, then from the five highest on the List the said House shall in like Manner choose the President. But in choosing the President, the Votes shall be taken by States, the Representation from each State having one Vote; a quorum for this Purpose shall consist of a Member or Members from two-thirds of the States, and a Majority of all the States shall be necessary to a Choice. In every Case, after the Choice of the President, the Person having the greatest Number of Votes of the Electors shall be the Vice President. But if there should remain two or more who have equal Votes, the Senate shall choose from them by Ballot the Vice President [Modified by Amendment XII].

The Congress may determine the Time of choosing the Electors, and the Day on which they shall give their Votes; which Day shall be the same throughout the United States.

No Person except a natural born Citizen, or a Citizen of the United States, at the time of the Adoption of this Constitution, shall be eligible to the Office of President; neither shall any Person be eligible to that Office who shall not have attained to the Age of thirty-five Years, and been fourteen Years a Resident within the United States.

In Case of the Removal of the President from Office, or of his Death, Resignation, or

Inability to discharge the Powers and Duties of the said Office, the Same shall devolve on the Vice President, and the Congress may by Law provide for the Case of Removal, Death, Resignation or Inability, both of the President and Vice President, declaring what Officer shall then act as President, and such Officer shall act accordingly, until the Disability be removed, or a President shall be elected [Modified by Amendment XXV].

The President shall, at stated Times, receive for his Services, a Compensation, which shall neither be increased nor diminished during the Period for which he shall have been elected, and he shall not receive within that Period any other Emolument from the United States, or any of them.

Before he enter on the Execution of his Office, he shall take the following Oath or Affirmation:— "I do solemnly swear (or affirm) that I will faithfully execute the Office of President of the United States, and will to the best of my Ability, preserve, protect and defend the Constitution of the United States."

Section 2. The President shall be Commander in Chief of the Army and Navy of the United States, and of the Militia of the several States, when called into the actual Service of the United States; he may require the Opinion, in writing, of the principal Officer in each of the executive Departments, upon any Subject relating to the Duties of their respective Offices, and he shall have Power to grant Reprieves and Pardons for Offenses against the United States, except in Cases of Impeachment.

He shall have Power, by and with the Advice and Consent of the Senate, to make Treaties, provided two-thirds of the Senators present concur; and he shall nominate, and by and with the Advice and Consent of the Senate, shall appoint Ambassadors, other public Ministers and Consuls, Judges of the supreme Court, and all other Officers of the United States, whose Appointments are not herein otherwise provided for, and which shall be established by Law: but the Congress may by Law vest the Appointment of such inferior Officers, as they think proper, in the President alone, in the Courts of Law, or in the Heads of Departments.

The President shall have Power to fill up all Vacancies that may happen during the Recess of the Senate, by granting Commissions which shall expire at the End of their next Session.

Section 3. He shall from time to time give to the Congress Information of the State of the Union, and recommend to their Consideration such Measures as he shall judge necessary and expedient; he may, on extraordinary Occasions, convene both Houses, or either of them, and in Case of Disagreement between them, with Respect to the Time of Adjournment, he may adjourn them to such Time as he shall think proper; he shall receive Ambassadors and other public Ministers;

he shall take Care that the Laws be faithfully executed, and shall Commission all the Officers of the United States.

Section 4. The President, Vice President and all civil Officers of the United States, shall be removed from Office on Impeachment for, and Conviction of, Treason, Bribery, or other high Crimes and Misdemeanors.

ARTICLE III.

Section 1. The judicial Power of the United States shall be vested in one Supreme Court, and in such inferior Courts as the Congress may from time to time ordain and establish. The Judges, both of the supreme and inferior Courts, shall hold their Offices during good Behavior, and shall, at stated Times, receive for their Services, a Compensation, which shall not be diminished during their Continuance in Office.

Section 2. The judicial Power shall extend to all Cases, in Law and Equity, arising under this Constitution, the Laws of the United States, and Treaties made, or which shall be made, under their Authority;—to all Cases affecting Ambassadors, other public Ministers and Consuls;—to all Cases of admiralty and maritime Jurisdiction;—to Controversies to which the United States shall be a Party;—to Controversies between two or more States;—between a State and Citizens of another State [Modified by Amendment XI];—between Citizens of different States;—between Citizens of the same State claiming Lands under Grants of different States, and between a State, or the Citizens thereof, and foreign States, Citizens or Subjects.

In all Cases affecting Ambassadors, other public Ministers and Consuls, and those in which a State shall be a Party, the Supreme Court shall have original Jurisdiction. In all the other Cases before mentioned, the Supreme Court shall have appellate Jurisdiction, both as to Law and Fact, with such Exceptions, and under such Regulations as the Congress shall make.

The Trial of all Crimes, except in Cases of Impeachment, shall be by Jury; and such Trial shall be held in the State where the said Crimes shall have been committed; but when not committed within any State, the Trial shall be at such Place or Places as the Congress may by Law have directed.

Section 3. Treason against the United States, shall consist only in levying War against them, or in adhering to their Enemies, giving them Aid and Comfort. No Person shall be convicted of Treason unless on the Testimony of two Witnesses to the same overt Act, or on Confession in open Court.

The Congress shall have Power to declare the Punishment of Treason, but no Attainder of Treason shall work Corruption of Blood, or Forfeiture except during the Life of the Person attainted.

ARTICLE IV.

Section 1. Full Faith and Credit shall be given in each State to the public Acts, Records, and judicial Proceedings of every other State. And the Congress may by general Laws prescribe the Manner in which such Acts, Records and Proceedings shall be proved, and the Effect thereof.

Section 2. The Citizens of each State shall be entitled to all Privileges and Immunities of Citizens in the several States.

A Person charged in any State with Treason, Felony, or other Crime, who shall flee from Justice, and be found in another State, shall on Demand of the executive Authority of the State from which he fled, be delivered up, to be removed to the State having Jurisdiction of the Crime.

No Person held to Service or Labor in one State, under the Laws thereof, escaping into another, shall, in Consequence of any Law or Regulation therein, be discharged from such Service or Labor, but shall be delivered up on Claim of the Party to whom such Service or Labor may be due [Modified by Amendment XIII].

Section 3. New States may be admitted by the Congress into this Union; but no new State shall be formed or erected within the Jurisdiction of any other State; nor any State be formed by the Junction of two or more States, or Parts of States, without the Consent of the Legislatures of the States concerned as well as of the Congress.

The Congress shall have Power to dispose of and make all needful Rules and Regulations respecting the Territory or other Property belonging to the United States; and nothing in this Constitution shall be so construed as to Prejudice any Claims of the United States, or of any particular State.

Section 4. The United States shall guarantee to every State in this Union a Republican Form of Government, and shall protect each of them against Invasion; and on Application of the Legislature, or of the Executive (when the Legislature cannot be convened), against domestic Violence.

ARTICLE V.

The Congress, whenever two thirds of both Houses shall deem it necessary, shall propose Amendments to this Constitution, or on the Application of the Legislatures of two thirds of the several States, shall call a Convention for proposing Amendments, which, in either Case, shall be valid to all Intents and Purposes, as Part of this Constitution, when ratified by the Legislatures of three fourths of the several States, or by Conventions in three fourths thereof, as the one or the other Mode of Ratification may be proposed by the Congress; Provided that no Amendment which may be made prior to the Year One thousand eight hundred and eight shall in any Manner affect the first and fourth Clauses in the Ninth Section of the First Article; and that no State, without its Consent, shall be deprived of its equal Suffrage in the Senate [Possibly abrogated by Amendment XVII].

ARTICLE VI.

All Debts contracted and Engagements entered into, before the Adoption of this Constitution, shall be as valid against the United States under this Constitution, as under the Confederation.

This Constitution, and the Laws of the United States which shall be made in Pursuance thereof; and all Treaties made, or which shall be made, under the Authority of the United States, shall be the supreme Law of the Land; and the Judges in every State shall be bound thereby, any Thing in the Constitution or Laws of any State to the Contrary notwithstanding.

The Senators and Representatives before mentioned, and the Members of the several State Legislatures, and all executive and judicial Officers, both of the United States and of the several States, shall be bound by Oath or Affirmation, to support this Constitution; but no religious Test shall ever be required as a Qualification to any Office or public Trust under the United States.

ARTICLE VII.

The Ratification of the Conventions of nine States shall be sufficient for the Establishment of this Constitution between the States so ratifying the Same.

This painting shows an idealized view of the delegates debating, as they did throughout the long, hot Philadelphia summer of 1787. Even George Washington (standing right) said that he saw no end in sight. Finally, in mid-September, the weary delegates signed the final document.

This 1788 cartoon shows the nine states that first ratified the Constitution as pillars supporting the arch of government. The pillars representing Virginia and New York have not yet been erected because these two states had not yet ratified the document.

The Ninth PILLAR *erected* !

" The Ratification of the Conventions of nine States, shall be sufficient for the establishment of this Constitution, between the States so ratifying the same." *Art.* vii.

INCIPIENT MAGNI PROCEDERE MENSES.

☞If it is not up it will rise.

The Attraction must be irresistible

In his final speech to the delegates, Benjamin Franklin said, "I consent, Sir, to this Constitution, because I expect no better, and because I am not sure that it is not the best."

Because they were serving as ambassadors in Europe, Thomas Jefferson and John Adams did not attend the Philadelphia meeting. But Jefferson praised the delegates as "an assembly of demigods."

At just 4,440 words, the U.S. Constitution is the shortest document of its kind. It is also the oldest.

The very first line of the Constitution establishes the source of the government's authority in the United States: "We the People . . ."

The last page of the Constitution contains the signatures, organized by state.

In the eighteenth century, Independence Hall (or the State House) in Philadelphia was the site of several important assemblies opposing British policies. In addition to the Constitutional Convention in 1787, the Second Continental Congress met at Independence Hall in 1775, and the Declaration of Independence was signed there in 1776.

The original Constitution is on display at the National Archives in Washington, D.C., along with the Declaration of Independence and the Bill of Rights.

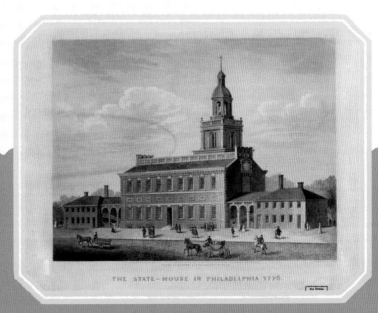

THE STATE-HOUSE IN PHILADELPHIA 1776.

Order of Proceffion,
In Honor of the Conftitution of the United States.

AT eight o'Clock on Wednefday Morning the 23d of July, 10 Guns will fire, when the PROCESSION will parade and proceed by the following Route, viz : Down Broad-Way to Great-Dock-Street, thence through Hanover-Square, Queen, Chatham, Divifion, and Arundel-Streets ; and from thence through Bullock-Street to Bayard's-Houfe.

No. 1.   2 Horfemen with Trumpets.
          1 piece of Artillery.

No.   Firft D I V I S I O N.

3   4 Forefters in Frocks, carrying Axes.   No.
4   Columbus in his Ancient Drefs—on Horfeback. 12   A Band of Mufic.
5   6 Forefters, &c.   13   Taylors.
6   A Plough.   14   Meafurers of Grain.
7   A Sower.   15   Millers.
8   A Harrow.   16   Infpectors of Flour.
9   Farmers.   17   Bakers.
10   United States Arms, borne by Col. White, fupported 18   Brewers.
11   Gardeners.   [by the Society of the Cincinnati.   19   Diftillers.

                    Second D I V I S I O N.

20   Coopers.   22   Tanners and Curriers.
21   Butchers.   23   Leather Dreffers.

                    Third D I V I S I O N.

                                24   Cord Wainers.

                    Fourth D I V I S I O N.

25   Carpenters.   27   Hatters.
26   Fnurters.   28   Peruke-Makers and Hair-Dreffers.

                    Fifth D I V I S I O N.

29   White-Smiths.   35   Windfor-Chair-Makers.
30   Cutlers.   36   Upholfterers.
31   Stone Mafons.   37   Fringe Makers.
32   Brick-Layers.   38   Paper Strainers.
33   Painters and Glaziers.   39   Civil Engineers.
34   Cabinet Makers.

                    Sixth D I V I S I O N.

40   Ship-Wrights.   44   Block and Pump-Makers.
41   Black-Smiths.   45   Sail-Makers, and Rope-Makers.
42   Ship-Joiners.   46   Riggers.
43   Boat-Builders.

                    Seventh D I V I S I O N.

47   Federal Ship Hamilton.   50   Marine Society.
48   Pilot Boat and Barges.   51   Printers, Book-Binders and Stationers.
49   Pilots.

                    Eighth D I V I S I O N.

52   Cartmen.   60   Gold and Silver-Smiths.
53   Mathematical Inftrument-Makers.   61   Potters.
54   Carvers and Engravers.   62   Chocolate-Makers.
55   Coach-Makers.   63   Tobacconifts.
56   Coach-Painters.   64   Dyers.
57   Copper-Smiths and Brafs-Founders.   65   Brufh-Makers.
58   Tin-plate Workers.   66   Tallow-Chandlers.
59   Pewterers.   67   Saddlers, Harnefs and Whip-Makers.

                    Ninth D I V I S I O N.

68   Gentlemen of the Bar.   70   Prefident and Students of the College.
69   Philological Society.   71   Merchants and Traders.

                    Tenth D I V I S I O N.

                                72   Clergy.
                                73   Phyficians.
                                74   Strangers.
                                75   Military Officers.
                                76   1 piece of Artillery.

By Order of the Committee of Arrangements,
RICHARD PLATT, Chairman.

When the Constitution was finally ratified, there was a great celebration in New York City. This program, titled "Order of Procession in Honor of the Constitution of the United States," lists the order in which people would march in the parade, as well as the route to be taken through the city.

THE BILL OF RIGHTS

AMENDMENT I

Congress shall make no law respecting an establishment of religion, or prohibiting the free exercise thereof; or abridging the freedom of speech, or of the press; or the right of the people peaceably to assemble, and to petition the Government for a redress of grievances.

AMENDMENT II

A well regulated Militia, being necessary to the security of a free State, the right of the people to keep and bear Arms, shall not be infringed.

AMENDMENT III

No Soldier shall, in time of peace, be quartered in any house, without the consent of the Owner, nor in time of war, but in a manner to be prescribed by law.

AMENDMENT IV

The right of the people to be secure in their persons, houses, papers, and effects, against unreasonable searches and seizures, shall not be violated, and no Warrants shall issue, but upon probable cause, supported by Oath or affirmation, and particularly describing the place to be searched, and the persons or things to be seized.

AMENDMENT V

No person shall be held to answer for a capital or otherwise infamous crime, unless on a presentment or indictment of a Grand Jury, except in cases arising in the land or naval forces, or in the Militia, when in actual service in time of War or public danger; nor shall any person be subject for the same offence to be twice put in jeopardy of life or limb; nor shall be compelled in any criminal case to be a witness against himself, nor be deprived of life, liberty, or property, without due process of law; nor shall private property be taken for public use, without just compensation.

AMENDMENT VI

In all criminal prosecutions, the accused shall enjoy the right to a speedy and public trial, by an impartial jury of the State and district wherein the crime shall have been committed, which district shall have been previously ascertained by law, and to be informed of the nature and cause of the accusation; to be confronted with the witnesses against him; to have compulsory process for obtaining witnesses in his favor, and to have the Assistance of Counsel for his defence.

AMENDMENT VII

In suits at common law, where the value in controversy shall exceed twenty dollars, the right of trial by jury shall be preserved, and no fact tried by a jury, shall be otherwise reexamined in any Court of the United States, than according to the rules of the common law.

AMENDMENT VIII

Excessive bail shall not be required, nor excessive fines imposed, nor cruel and unusual punishments inflicted.

AMENDMENT IX

The enumeration in the Constitution, of certain rights, shall not be construed to deny or disparage others retained by the people.

AMENDMENT X

The powers not delegated to the United States by the Constitution, nor prohibited by it to the States, are reserved to the States respectively, or to the people. ★

James Madison had to work hard to get Congress to pass the Bill of Rights. Some members, like Alexander Hamilton, thought these rights were already protected in the Constitution, and so the Bill was unnecessary. Others, who opposed a strong national government and hoped to cripple its powers, fought against passage. In the end, however, popular support helped persuade Congress to approve the first 10 amendments.

One of the two amendments the states did not ratify dealt with the number of representatives in Congress. The other amendment that the states refused to approve became the Twenty-seventh Amendment in 1992. This amendment prevents Congress from passing immediate salary increases for itself. It says, "No law varying the compensation for the services of the senators and representatives shall take effect, until an election of representatives shall have intervened." It took more than 202 years to ratify this amendment!

In the Bill of Rights, the Tenth Amendment was the only one that did not protect individual rights. Madison included it to calm the many people who still feared that the new government would have too much power over the states.

AUTHORS

Most of the 55 delegates to the Constitutional Convention were merchants, planters, and lawyers. Many of the nation's founding fathers were represented, including George Washington, Alexander Hamilton, James Madison, and Benjamin Franklin. Of all the Constitution's framers, or writers, Madison (1751–1836) made the most significant contribution. For this he is called the Father of the Constitution. Advised by Jefferson, he wrote the Bill of Rights during the first term of Congress. He later served as Secretary of State for Jefferson and, in 1809, was elected the fourth president and served two terms.

In 1804 the states ratified two more amendments. No more amendments were added for the next 60 years.

RESPONSE

A great national debate arose over the ratification of the Constitution during the fall and winter of 1787 and 1788. Many worried about the centralized government having too much power, preferring power to be in the hands of the states. However, on June 21, New Hampshire became the ninth state to ratify it, establishing the Constitution as the law of the land. Within two years, Rhode Island, the remaining state, had ratified it.

Passing the Bill of Rights was difficult as well. Six months after its submission, 9 out of the 10 states needed for approval had ratified. But then everything stalled. For various reasons, Virginia, Georgia, and Connecticut held out. It wasn't until Vermont was admitted to the Union in 1791 that another state ratified the Bill of Rights. Virginia quickly followed Vermont's lead and the Bill of Rights became an essential part of the Constitution.

The Bill of Rights guaranteed that Americans would have basic rights such as freedom of speech, religion, and the press.

FAREWELL ADDRESS

GEORGE WASHINGTON

September 19, 1796

At the end of two terms, a weary George Washington decided to retire from the office of President of the United States. In his Farewell Address, he appealed for national unity, warning against sectional conflict. Alarmed by the bitter rivalry between the two political parties, Federalists and Republicans, he cautioned against political strife. In the second, and most famous, part of his address, he urged the United States to develop its foreign trade but make no permanent alliances with other nations. This advice guided United States foreign policy until the twentieth century.

FAREWELL ADDRESS

The period for a new election of a citizen to administer the executive government of the United States being not far distant, and the time actually arrived when your thoughts must be employed in designating the person who is to be clothed with that important trust, it appears to me proper, especially as it may conduce to a more distinct expression of the public voice, that I should now apprise you of the resolution I have formed to decline being considered among the number of those out of whom a choice is to be made. . . .

The unity of government which constitutes you one people is also now dear to you. It is justly so, for it is a main pillar in the edifice of your real independence, the support of your tranquility at home, your peace abroad, of your safety, of your prosperity, of that very liberty which you so highly prize. But as it is easy to foresee that from different causes and from different quarters much pains will be taken, many artifices employed, to weaken in your minds the conviction of this truth, as this is the point in your political fortress against which the batteries of internal and external enemies will be most constantly and actively (though often covertly and insidiously) directed, it is of infinite moment that you should properly estimate the immense value of your national union to your collective and individual happiness; that you should cherish a cordial, habitual, and immovable attachment to it; accustoming yourselves to think and speak of it as of the palladium of your political safety and prosperity; watching for its preservation with jealous anxiety; discountenancing whatever may suggest even a suspicion that it can in any event be abandoned, and indignantly frowning upon the first dawning of every attempt to alienate any portion of our country from the rest or to enfeeble the sacred ties which now link together the various parts.

For this you have every inducement of sympathy and interest. Citizens by birth or choice of a common country, that country has a right to concentrate your affections. The name of American, which belongs to you in your national capacity, must always exalt the just pride of patriotism more than any appellation derived from local discriminations. With slight shades of difference, you have the same religion, manners, habits, and political principles. You have in a common cause fought and triumphed together. The independence and liberty you possess are the work of joint councils and joint efforts, of common dangers, sufferings, and successes. . . .

In contemplating the causes which may disturb our union it occurs as matter of serious concern that any ground should have been furnished for characterizing parties by geographical

━━▶

discriminations—Northern and Southern, Atlantic and Western—whence designing men may endeavor to excite a belief that there is a real difference of local interests and views. One of the expedients of party to acquire influence within particular districts is to misrepresent the opinions and aims of other districts. You can not shield yourselves too much against the jealousies and heartburnings which spring from these mis-representations; they tend to render alien to each other those who ought to be bound together by fraternal affection. . . .

To the efficacy and permanency of your union a government for the whole is indispensable. No alliances, however strict, between the parts can be an adequate substitute. They must inevitably experience the infractions and interruptions which all alliances in all times have experienced. Sensible of this momen-tous truth, you have improved upon your first essay by the adoption of a Constitution of government better calculated than your former for an intimate union and for the efficacious management of your common concerns. This government, the offspring of our own choice, uninfluenced and unawed, adopted upon full investigation and mature deliberation, completely free in its principles, in the distribution of its powers, uniting security with energy, and containing within itself a provision for its own amendment, has a just claim to your confidence and your support. Respect for its authority, compliance with its laws, acquies-cence in its measures, are duties enjoined by the fundamental maxims of true liberty. The basis of our political systems is the right of the people to make and to alter their constitutions of government. But the constitution which at any time exists till changed by an explicit and authentic act of the whole people is sacredly obligatory upon all. The very idea of the power and the right of the people to establish government presupposes the duty of every individual to obey the established government. . . .

Toward the preservation of your government and the permanency of your present happy state, it is requisite not only that you steadily discountenance irregular oppositions to its acknowledged authority, but also that you resist with care the spirit of innovation upon its principles, however specious the pretexts. One method of assault may be to effect in the forms of the Constitution alterations which will impair the energy of the system, and thus to undermine what can not be directly overthrown. In all the changes to which you may be invited remember that time and habit are at least as necessary to fix the true character of governments as of other human institutions; that experience is the surest standard by which to test the real tendency of the exist-ing constitution of a country; that facility in changes upon the credit of mere hypothesis and opinion exposes to perpetual change, from the endless variety of hypothesis and opinion; and remember especially that for the efficient management of your common interests in a country so extensive as ours a government of as much vigor as is consistent with the perfect security of liberty is indispensable. . . .

I have already intimated to you the danger of parties in the state, with particular reference to the founding of them on geographical discriminations. Let me now take a more comprehensive view, and warn you in the most solemn manner against the baneful effects of the spirit of party generally.

This spirit, unfortunately, is inseparable from our nature, having its root in the strongest passions of the human mind. It exists under different shapes in all governments, more or less stifled, controlled, or repressed; but in those of the popular form it is seen in its greatest rankness and is truly their worst enemy. . . .

It serves always to distract the public councils and enfeeble the public administration. It agitates the community with illfounded jealousies and false alarms; kindles the animosity of one part against another; foments occasionally riot and insurrection. It opens the door to foreign influence and corruption, which find a facilitated access to the government itself through the channels of party passion. Thus the policy and the will of one country are subjected to the policy and will of another. . . .

Of all the dispositions and habits which lead to political prosperity, religion and morality are indispensable supports. In vain would that man claim the tribute of patriotism who should labor to subvert these great pillars of human happiness—these firmest props of the duties of men and citizens. The mere politician, equally with the pious man, ought to respect and to cherish them. A volume could not trace all their connections with private and public felicity. Let it simply be asked, Where is the security for property, for reputation, for life, if the sense of religious obligation desert the oaths which are the instruments of investigation in courts of justice? And let us with caution indulge the supposition that morality can be maintained without religion. Whatever may be conceded to the influence of refined education on minds of peculiar structure, reason and experience both forbid us to expect that national morality can prevail in exclusion of religious principle.

It is substantially true that virtue or morality is a necessary spring of popular government. The rule indeed extends with more or less force to every species of free government. Who that is a sincere friend to it can look with indifference upon attempts to shake the foundation of the fabric? Promote, then, as an object of primary importance, institutions for the general diffusion of knowledge. In proportion as the structure of a government gives force to public opinion, it is essential that public opinion should be enlightened.

As a very important source of strength and security, cherish public credit. One method of preserving it is to use it as sparingly as possible, avoiding occasions of expense by cultivating peace, but remembering also that timely disbursements to prepare for danger frequently prevent much greater disbursements to repel it; avoiding likewise the accumulation of debt, not only by shunning of expense, but by vigorous exertions in time of peace to discharge the debts which unavoidable wars have occasioned, not ungenerously throwing upon prosperity the burden which we ourselves ought to bear. . . .

Against the insidious wiles of foreign influence (I conjure you to believe me, fellow-citizens) the jealousy of a free people ought to be constantly awake, since history and experience prove that foreign influence is one of the most baneful foes of republican government. But that jealousy, to be useful, must be impartial, else it becomes the instrument of the very influence to be avoided, instead of a defense against it. Excessive partiality for one foreign nation and excessive dislike of another cause those whom that actuate to see danger only on one side, and serve to veil and even second the arts of influence on the other. Real patriots who may resist the intrigues of the favorite are liable to become suspected and odious, while its tools and dupes usurp the applause and confidence of the people to surrender their interests.

The great rule of conduct for us in regard to foreign nations is, in extending our commercial relations to have with them as little political connection as possible. So far as we have already formed engagements let them be fulfilled with perfect good faith. Here let us stop.

Europe has a set of primary interests which to us have none or a very remote relation. Hence she must be engaged in frequent controversies, the causes of which are essentially foreign to our concerns. Hence, therefore, it must be unwise in us to implicate ourselves to artificial ties in the ordinary vicissitudes of her politics or the ordinary combinations and collisions of her friendships or enmities.

Our detached and distant situation invites and enables us to pursue a different course. If we remain one people, under an efficient government, the period is not far off when we may defy material injury from external annoyance; when we may take such an attitude as will cause the neutrality we may at any time resolve upon to be scrupulously respected; when belligerent nations, under the impossibility of making acquisitions upon us, will not lightly hazard the giving us provocation; when we may choose peace or war, as our interest, guided by justice, shall counsel.

Why forego the advantages of so peculiar a situation? Why quit our own to stand upon foreign ground? Why, by interweaving our destiny with that of any part of Europe, entangle our peace and prosperity in the toils of European ambition, rivalship, interest, humor, or caprice? . . .

Though in reviewing the incidents of my administration I am unconscious of intentional error, I am nevertheless too sensible of my defects not to think it probable that I may have committed many errors. Whatever they may be, I fervently beseech the Almighty to avert or mitigate the evils to which they may tend. I shall also carry with me the hope that my country will never cease to view them with indulgence, and that, after forty-five years of my life dedicated to its service with an upright zeal, the faults of incompetent abilities will be consigned to oblivion, as myself must soon be to the mansions of rest.

Relying on its kindness in this as in other things, and actuated by that fervent love toward it which is so natural to a man who views in it the native soil of himself and his progenitors for several generations, I anticipate with pleasing expectation that retreat in which I promise myself to realize without alloy the sweet enjoyment of partaking in the midst of my fellow citizens the benign influence of good laws under a free government—the ever-favorite object of my heart, and the happy reward, as I trust, of our mutual cares, labors, and dangers. ★

The nation's first president, George Washington, says an emotional farewell to his officers at the end of his presidency.

George Washington delivered the Farewell Address to his cabinet, and it was published in the newspapers the next day. Every year since 1896, the address has been read on the floor of the U.S. Senate on Washington's birthday.

Washington's warning

against "entangling alliances" with other nations became known as the "Great Rule." The "Great Rule" guided American foreign policy until 1917, when the United States declared war against Germany.

In entering World War I, America allied herself with three great European powers—Britain, France, and Russia.

After completing two terms as president, Washington wanted to retire. He refused to be considered for a third term and returned home to Virginia to his beloved plantation, Mount Vernon. It had been his home for 45 years, and Washington took great pride in the land and buildings.

George Washington's wife, Martha, was not entirely comfortable in the role of first lady: Though she entertained often and was a hospitable hostess, she longed to return to Mount Vernon, away from the public life. While Washington was president, Martha wrote to a niece, confiding in her that she would "much rather be at home."

Official presidential residences were not provided for the nation's earliest leaders. The first presidential mansion was Washington's home in New York City—No. 1 Cherry Street—where he lived from 1789 to 1790.

James Madison had drafted the original version of Washington's Farewell Address in 1792, but Alexander Hamilton, Washington's Treasury Secretary and chief aide, was the architect of the final draft. Washington made some changes, but the text he read was in large part Hamilton's.

AUTHOR

George Washington (1732–1799) had reluctantly agreed to a second term as the nation's first president. By its end, he was in ill health and longing to return to private life. So he firmly rejected the offer of a third term.

Americans loved, respected, and admired their first president throughout his life, even after his retirement. This portrait of Washington in his old age captures his directness and dignity.

RESPONSE

Washington hoped his address would reduce political fighting, but the two parties ignored his warnings. By the end of the 1796 presidential campaign, political passions had flared as hot as ever. Republicans and Federalists routinely attacked each other privately and in the press. Still, in a world in which the expectation was that rulers would hold on to power until they were forced to give it up, Washington's gracious and voluntary farewell carried a great deal of weight. John Adams succeeded Washington as president. Washington's recommended policy of neutrality remained an influential part of American foreign policy for more than a century.

Numerous towns, cities, bridges, parks, and monuments have been named for George Washington, not to mention one state and our nation's capital. His image can be found printed on the one-dollar bill, engraved on the quarter and the Purple Heart, and carved on Mount Rushmore.

The nation was deeply saddened by Washington's death on December, 14, 1798. Cavalry general Henry Lee delivered the funeral oration. He said that Washington was "First in war, first in peace and first in the hearts of his countrymen. . . ."

THE STAR-SPANGLED BANNER

FRANCIS SCOTT KEY

September 16, 1814

Francis Scott Key wrote "The Star-Spangled Banner" during the War of 1812 between England and the United States. In September 1814, English troops entered Washington, D.C., and set fire to most of the government buildings. During their withdrawal from the city, they captured a friend of Key's. Soon afterward, Key and a government official sailed to the British fleet in Maryland's Chesapeake Bay to try to negotiate his friend's release. The British agreed to let the man go, but they were about to attack Baltimore and detained the Americans until after the attack. So Key and the government official sailed with the British, and, on September 13, they watched them fire on Fort McHenry, near Baltimore's harbor.

The bombardment lasted most of the night. At dawn, Key was overjoyed to see the fort was still flying the American flag. He began scribbling a few lines describing the bombardment. After Key returned to Baltimore, he completed his song.

THE STAR-SPANGLED BANNER

Oh, say, can you see, by the dawn's early light,
What so proudly we hailed at the twilight's last gleaming,
Whose broad stripes and bright stars through the perilous fight,
O'er the ramparts we watched were so gallantly streaming?
And the rockets' red glare, the bombs bursting in air,
Gave proof thro' the night that our flag was still there.
Oh, say, does that star-spangled banner yet wave
O'er the land of the free, and the home of the brave!

On the shore, dimly seen thro' the mists of the deep,
Where the foe's haughty host in dread silence reposes,
What is that which the breeze o'er the towering steep,
As it fitfully blows, half conceals, half discloses?
Now it catches the gleam of the morning's first beam,
In full glory reflected, now shines on the stream.
'Tis the star-spangled banner; oh, long may it wave
O'er the land of the free, and the home of the brave!

And where is that band who so vauntingly swore
That the havoc of war and the battle's confusion
A home and a country should leave us no more?

Their blood has washed out their foul footsteps' pollution.
No refuge could save the hireling and slave
From the terror of flight, or the gloom of the grave:
And the star-spangled banner in triumph doth wave
O'er the land of the free, and the home of the brave! ★

On January 8, 1815, Americans led by General Andrew Jackson (shown raising his sword in victory) defeated the British at the Battle of New Orleans. Jackson thought the battle ended the War of 1812, but the United States and Great Britain had signed a peace treaty a few days earlier in Europe. The armies gathered at New Orleans did not receive news of the peace treaty until after the battle.

This view of the bombardment of Fort McHenry shows the "bombs bursting in air" that Key described in "The Star-Spangled Banner."

AUTHOR

Born to a prosperous Maryland family, Francis Scott Key (1779–1843) was a well-known lawyer. He served as District Attorney for the District of Columbia from 1833 to 1841. Key, a slaveholder, was a founder of the American Colonization Society. This organization sought to phase out slavery by giving freed slaves the means to live in colonies in Africa (mostly Liberia). Key wrote poetry as a hobby throughout his life.

RESPONSE

Several days after the bombardment, Key's poem, "Defence of Fort McHenry," appeared on printed notices and was circulated around Baltimore. Soon it was published under the title "The Star-Spangled Banner." Shortly afterward, it became popular in other American cities.

Francis Scott Key's poem "The Star-Spangled Banner" was adopted as the United States's national anthem in 1931.

The people of Baltimore

quickly began singing Key's words, to the popular British tune, "To Anacreon in Heaven." Anacreon was a poet in ancient Greece known for his praise of love and wine. When Americans sing "The Star Spangled Banner," we're singing to the tune of an old British drinking song!

The flag that Key saw

flying over Fort McHenry covers one wall of the Smithsonian Institution's Museum of American History in Washington, D.C.

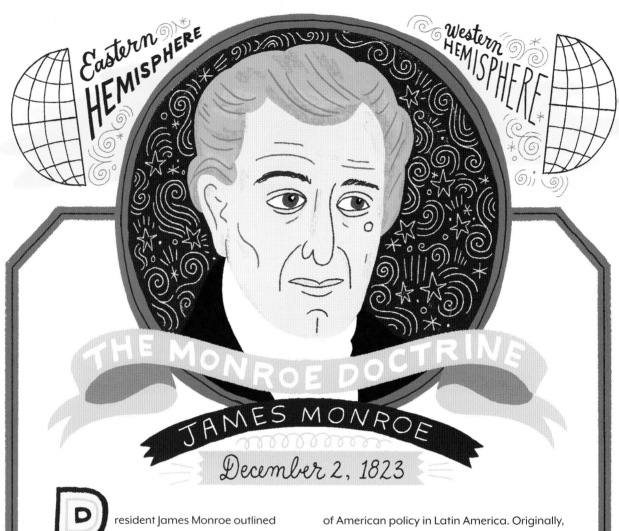

Eastern HEMISPHERE

Western HEMISPHERE

THE MONROE DOCTRINE

JAMES MONROE

December 2, 1823

President James Monroe outlined what is now known as the Monroe Doctrine in a speech to Congress. The president warned European nations that the Americas were off-limits for colonization. Monroe was responding to attempts by European powers to reassert control over former Latin American colonies, not to mention as yet unsettled areas of North America. By 1822, Argentina, Colombia, and Mexico, all once Spanish colonies, had rebelled against Spain and declared their independence.

Monroe's brief statement has guided much of American policy in Latin America. Originally, the doctrine had been intended to support weak Latin American countries against great powers and discourage Russian interference along the Pacific Northwest Coast. But as the United States grew more powerful, the U.S. government often used the Monroe Doctrine to justify its own interference in Latin American affairs. Many nations to the south grew resentful. In the late 1920s the United States began offering economic assistance to its Latin American neighbors, in effect adding a "carrot" to the "stick" of the Monroe Doctrine.

THE MONROE DOCTRINE

. . . At the proposal of the Russian Imperial Government, made through the minister of the Emperor residing here, a full power and instructions have been transmitted to the minister of the United States at St. Petersburg to arrange by amicable negotiation the respective rights and interests of the two nations on the northwest coast of this continent. A similar proposal had been made by his Imperial Majesty to the Government of Great Britain, which has likewise been acceded to. The Government of the United States has been desirous by this friendly proceeding of manifesting the great value which they have invariably attached to the friendship of the Emperor and their solicitude to cultivate the best understanding with his Government. In the discussions to which this interest has given rise and in the arrangements by which they may terminate, the occasion has been judged proper for asserting, as a principle in which the rights and interests of the United States are involved, that the American continents, by the free and independent condition which they have assumed and maintain, are henceforth not to be considered as subjects for future colonization by any Europeans powers. . . .

. . . In the wars of the European powers in matters relating to themselves we have never taken any part, nor does it comport with our policy so to do. It is only when our rights are invaded or seriously menaced that we resent injuries or make preparation for our defense. With the movements in this hemisphere we are of necessity more immediately connected, and by causes which must be obvious to all enlightened and impartial observers. The political system of the allied powers is essentially different in this respect from that of America. This difference proceeds from that which exists in their respective Governments; and between those new Governments and Spain we declared our neutrality at the time of their recognition, and to this we have adhered, and shall continue to adhere, provided no change shall occur which, in the judgment of the competent authorities of this Government, shall make a corresponding change on the part of the United States indispensable to their security.

The late events in Spain and Portugal show that Europe is still unsettled. Of this important fact no stronger proof can be adduced than that the allied powers should have thought it proper, on any principle satisfactory to themselves, to have interposed by force in the internal concerns of Spain. To what extent such interposition may be carried, on the same principle, is a question in which all independent powers whose governments differ from theirs are interested, even those most remote, and surely none more so than the United States. Our policy in regard to Europe, which was adopted at an early stage of the wars which have so long agitated that quarter of the globe, nevertheless remains the same, which is, not to interfere in the internal concerns of any of its powers; to consider the government de facto as the legitimate government for us; to cultivate friendly relations with it, and to preserve those relations by a frank, firm, and manly policy, meeting in all instances the just claims of every power, submitting to injuries from none. But in regard to those continents circumstances are eminently and conspicuously different. It is impossible that the allied powers should extend their political system to any portion of either continent without endangering our peace and happiness; nor can anyone believe that our southern brethren, if left to themselves, would adopt it of their own accord. It is equally impossible, therefore, that we should behold such interposition in any form with indifference. If we look to the comparative strength and resources of Spain and those new Governments, and their distance from each other, it must be obvious that she can never subdue them. It is still the true policy of the United States to leave the parties to themselves, in the hope that other powers will pursue the same course. . . . ★

In 1842 President John Tyler used this doctrine to justify taking Texas from Mexico. A Venezuelan newspaper then warned other Latin American countries against the United States: "Beware, brother, the wolf approaches the lambs."

AUTHOR

James Monroe (1758–1831) was the fifth president of the United States (1817–1825). The last of the founding fathers to serve as president, he was an excellent administrator. During Monroe's second term, Secretary of State John Quincy Adams (1767–1848) did not want to make enemies of the European powers, but he also did not want the foreign policy of the United States to be controlled by them. He influenced Monroe to pursue a new, more assertive American policy for the Western Hemisphere that later became known as the Monroe Doctrine. Adams became Monroe's successor as President of the United States.

RESPONSE

The American people praised Monroe's statement. But the European powers did not take Monroe's warning seriously. In 1823 the United States was not yet a world power. It lacked the military and economic strength to keep European countries out of Latin America. Yet by playing the European powers off of one another, the United States effectively enforced the doctrine until it became a world power. Russian settlement in the continental U.S. was never really a threat. The United States purchased Alaska from Russia in 1867.

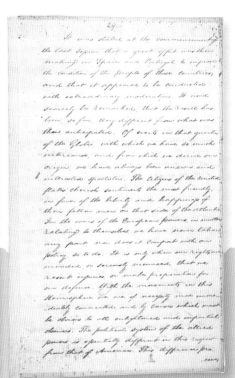

A photograph from the National Archives shows two pages of Monroe's message to Congress, which became the basis of the Monroe Doctrine. England shared the desire of the United States to keep Spain's power in check in Latin America. Without the power of Britain's navy behind it, the Monroe Doctrine would have been impossible for the United States to enforce alone.

DECLARATIONS of SENTIMENTS

SENECA FALLS CONVENTION

July 20, 1848

In 1848 American women had almost no legal rights. They could not own property or gain custody of their children in a divorce. They did not even have the right to vote. Two women, Lucretia Mott and Elizabeth Cady Stanton, organized a convention to discuss women's issues. Nearly three hundred people, mostly women, attended the meeting at Seneca Falls, New York, on July 19 and 20. There, they debated and adopted a "Declaration of Sentiments," which was deliberately modeled on the Declaration of Independence. In fact, it purposely used language that mimicked the original Declaration.

The Seneca Falls Convention was the first women's rights meeting in the United States. The Declaration of Sentiments launched the modern movement for gender equality. Feminists, as they became known, fought from then on to gain for women the same political, social, and legal rights enjoyed by men.

DECLARATION OF SENTIMENTS

When, in the course of human events, it becomes necessary for one portion of the family of man to assume among the people of the earth a position different from that which they have hitherto occupied, but one to which the laws of nature and of nature's God entitle them, a decent respect to the opinions of mankind requires that they should declare the causes that impel them to such a course.

We hold these truths to be self-evident: that all men and women are created equal; that they are endowed by their Creator with certain inalienable rights; that among these are life, liberty, and the pursuit of happiness; that to secure these rights governments are instituted, deriving their just powers from the consent of the governed. Whenever any form of government becomes destructive of these ends, it is the right of those who suffer from it to refuse allegiance to it, and to insist upon the institution of a new government, laying its foundation on such principles, and organizing its powers in such form, as to them shall seem most likely to effect their safety and happiness. Prudence, indeed, will dictate that governments long established should not be changed for light and transient causes; and accordingly all experience hath shown that mankind are more disposed to suffer, while evils are sufferable, than to right themselves by abolishing the forms to which they are accustomed. But when a long train of abuses and usurpations, pursuing invariably the same object evinces a design to reduce them under absolute despotism, it is their duty to throw off such government, and to provide new guards for their future security. Such has been the patient sufferance of the women under this government, and such is now the necessity which constrains them to demand the equal station to which they are entitled.

The history of mankind is a history of repeated injuries and usurpations on the part of man toward woman, having in direct object the establishment of an absolute tyranny over her. To prove this, let facts be submitted to a candid world.

He has never permitted her to exercise her inalienable right to the elective franchise.

He has compelled her to submit to laws, in the formation of which she had no voice.

He has withheld from her rights which are given to the most ignorant and degraded men—both natives and foreigners.

Having deprived her of this first right of a citizen, the elective franchise, thereby leaving her without representation in the halls of legislation, he has oppressed her on all sides.

He has made her, if married, in the eye of the law, civilly dead.

He has taken from her all right in property, even to the wages she earns.

He has made her, morally, an irresponsible being, as she can commit many crimes with impunity, provided they be done in the presence of her husband. In the covenant of marriage, she is compelled to promise obedience to her husband, he becoming, to all intents and purposes, her master—the law giving him power to deprive her of her liberty, and to administer chastisement.

He has so framed the laws of divorce, as to what shall be the proper causes and in case of separation, to whom the guardianship of the children shall be given, as to be wholly regardless of the happiness of women—the law, in all cases, going upon a false supposition of the supremacy of man, and giving all power into his hands.

After depriving her of all rights as a married woman, if single, and the owner of property, he has taxed her to support a government which recognizes her only when her property can be made profitable to it.

He has monopolized nearly all the profitable employments, and from those she is permitted to follow, she receives but a scanty remuneration. He closes against her all the avenues to wealth and distinction which he considers most honorable to himself. As a teacher of theology, medicine, or law, she is not known.

He has denied her the facilities for obtaining a thorough education, all colleges being closed against her.

He allows her in Church, as well as State, but a subordinate position, claiming Apostolic authority for her exclusion from the ministry, and, with some exceptions, from any public participation in the affairs of the Church.

He has created a false public sentiment by giving to the world a different code of morals for men and women, by which moral delinquencies which exclude women from society, are not only tolerated, but deemed of little account in man.

He has usurped the prerogative of Jehovah himself, claiming it as his right to assign for her a sphere of action, when that belongs to her conscience and to her God.

He has endeavored, in every way that he could, to destroy her confidence in her own powers, to lessen her self-respect and to make her willing to lead a dependent and abject life.

Now, in view of this entire disfranchisement of one-half the people of this country, their social and religious degradation—in view of the unjust laws above mentioned, and because women do feel themselves aggrieved, oppressed, and fraudulently deprived of their most sacred rights, we insist that they have immediate admission to all the rights and privileges which belong to them as citizens of the United States.

In entering upon the great work before us, we anticipate no small amount of misconception, misrepresentation, and ridicule; but we shall use every instrumentality within our power to effect our object. We shall employ agents, circulate tracts, petition the State and National legislatures, and endeavor to enlist the pulpit and the press in our behalf. We hope this Convention will be followed by a series of Conventions embracing every part of the country.

Firmly relying upon the final triumph of the Right and the True, we do this day affix our signatures to this declaration. . . .

Resolved, That such laws as conflict, in any way, with the true and substantial happiness of woman, are contrary to the great precept of nature, and of no validity: for this is "superior in obligation to any other."

Resolved, That all laws which prevent woman from occupying such a station in society as her conscience shall dictate, or which place her in a position inferior to that of man, are contrary to the great precept of nature, and therefore of no force or authority.

Resolved, That woman is man's equal—was intended to be so by the Creator, and the highest good of the race demands that she should be recognized as such.

Resolved, That the women of this country ought to be enlightened in regard to the laws under which they live, that they may no longer publish their degradation by declaring themselves satisfied with their present position, nor their ignorance, by asserting that they have all the rights they want.

Resolved, That inasmuch as man, while claiming for himself intellectual superiority, does accord to woman moral superiority, it is pre-eminently his duty to encourage her to speak and teach, as she has an opportunity, in all religious assemblies.

Resolved, That the same amount of virtue, delicacy, and refinement of behavior that is required of woman in the social state, should also be required of man, and the same transgressions should be visited with equal severity on both man and woman.

Resolved, That the objection of indelicacy and impropriety, which is so often brought against woman when she addresses a public audience, comes with a very ill-grace from those who encourage, by their attendance, her appearance on the stage, in the concert, or in feats of the circus.

Resolved, That woman has too long rested satisfied in the circumscribed limits which corrupt customs and a perverted application of the Scriptures have marked out for her, and that it is time she should move in the enlarged sphere which her great Creator has assigned her.

Resolved, That it is the duty of the women of this country to secure to themselves their sacred right to the elective franchise.

Resolved, That the equality of human rights results necessarily from the fact of the identity of the race in capabilities and responsibilities.

Resolved, That the speedy success of our cause depends upon the zealous and untiring efforts of both men and women, for the overthrow of the monopoly of the pulpit, and for the securing to women an equal participation with men in the various trades, professions, and commerce.

Resolved, therefore, That, being invested by the Creator with the same capabilities, and the same consciousness of responsibility for their exercise, it is demonstrably the right and duty of woman, equally with man, to promote every righteous cause by every righteous means; and especially in regard to the great subjects of morals and religion, it is self-evidently her right to participate with her brother in teaching them, both in private and in public, by writing and by speaking, by any instrumentalities proper to be used, and in any assemblies proper to be held; and this being a self-evident truth growing out of the divinely implanted principles of human nature, any custom or authority adverse to it, whether modern or wearing the hoary sanction of antiquity, is to be regarded as self-evident falsehood, and at war with the interests of mankind. ★

Elizabeth Cady Stanton was photographed with her eldest child, Daniel, in 1854. As a child Stanton spent time at her father's law practice. Several times she heard him explaining to women the laws that did not allow them to own property—experiences that later spurred her to action.

Though Mott and Stanton

organized the Seneca Falls convention in response to being barred from the floor at the 1840 World Anti-Slavery Convention, which didn't allow women, the Seneca Falls resolutions focused on the rights of white women only. In 1866, however, Stanton and Susan B. Anthony were involved in the formation of the American Equal Rights Association (AERA), an organization dedicated to enfranchising African-Americans and women together.

The few men who participated

in the convention were abolitionists. Abolitionists were people who worked for the immediate end, or abolition, of slavery in the United States. Frederick Douglass (see p. 80) was a speaker at the convention and a signer of its resolution.

AUTHORS

The Declaration of Sentiments represented the combined efforts of the women and men attending the convention. However, Lucretia Mott (1793–1880) and Elizabeth Cady Stanton (1815–1902) played key roles. Mott was an abolitionist and a women's suffragist. She went to London in 1840 for the World's Anti-Slavery Convention, but became infuriated when she was not allowed to attend because she was a woman. While in London she met Elizabeth Cady Stanton. Influenced by Mott, Stanton went on to become a leader of the women's rights movement. In 1869 Stanton helped found the first organization to champion a constitutional amendment giving women the right to vote.

RESPONSE

Most Americans in the mid-nineteenth century did not believe that women should have the same rights as men. So it was not surprising that the newspapers that reported the convention made fun of it. The *Oneida Whig* called it "the most shocking and unnatural incident ever recorded in the history of womanity"; John Tanner, publisher of *The Mechanic's Advocate* opined that a "true hearted female will instantly feel that it is unwomanly."

But the participants felt their meeting was a success, so they planned a second meeting three weeks later in Rochester, New York.

Susan B. Anthony, another advocate of women's rights, shown seated in her office in 1900. The photographs on Anthony's desk are of the many women who fought to promote women's suffrage. On a visit to Seneca Falls, three years after the convention, Anthony first met Elizabeth Cady Stanton. The two joined forces to lead the women's rights movement for the next 50 years.

During the Seneca Falls Convention, Elizabeth Cady Stanton introduced the resolution demanding that women have the right to vote. The resolution was approved. But because the idea of women voting was so far ahead of its time, it was the only resolution that did not pass unanimously. American women finally won the vote in 1920, with the passing of the Nineteenth Amendment to the Constitution (see p. 124).

A woman who attended the convention recalled, "At first we travelled quite alone. But before we had gone many miles we came on other wagon-loads of women, bound in the same direction."

(see p. 124)

THE MEANING OF THE FOURTH OF JULY FOR THE NEGRO

FREDERICK DOUGLASS

July 5, 1852

Frederick Douglass escaped from slavery in Maryland in 1838 and became a leading voice in the abolitionist movement in pre–Civil War America, especially after the 1845 publication of a memoir of his life in slavery and his escape from it. Douglass was the publisher of an abolitionist newspaper in Rochester, New York, when he delivered this speech to a full house in Rochester's Corinthian Hall.

Douglass brilliantly used the occasion of the Fourth of July to contrast the celebrations of freedom across the country with the widespread and terrible conditions of slavery. Douglass argues that the enslavement of Negroes is not only cruel, it is criminal—a blight on American ideals of freedom. Until slavery is abolished, said Douglass, Americans have no cause to celebrate the rights of man and individual liberty, let alone claim to set an example for the rest of the world.

THE MEANING OF THE FOURTH OF JULY FOR THE NEGRO

What, to the American slave, is your 4th of July? I answer; a day that reveals to him, more than all other days in the year, the gross injustice and cruelty to which he is the constant victim. To him, your celebration is a sham; your boasted liberty, an unholy license; your national greatness, swelling vanity; your sounds of rejoicing are empty and heartless; your denunciation of tyrants, brass fronted impudence; your shouts of liberty and equality, hollow mockery; your prayers and hymns, your sermons and thanksgivings, with all your religious parade and solemnity, are, to Him, mere bombast, fraud, deception, impiety, and hypocrisy—a thin veil to cover up crimes which would disgrace a nation of savages. There is not a nation on the earth guilty of practices more shocking and bloody than are the people of the United States, at this very hour.

Go where you may, search where you will, roam through all the monarchies and despotisms of the Old World, travel through South America, search out every abuse, and when you have found the last, lay your facts by the side of the everyday practices of this nation, and you will say with me, that, for revolting barbarity and shameless hypocrisy, America reigns without a rival...

Behold the practical operation of this internal slave-trade, the American slave-trade, sustained by American politics and American religion. Here you will see men and women reared like swine for the market. You know what is a swine-drover? I will show you a man-drover. They inhabit all our Southern States. They perambulate the country, and crowd the highways of the nation, with droves of human stock. You will see one of these human flesh jobbers, armed with pistol, whip, and bowie-knife, driving a company of a hundred men, women, and children, from the Potomac to the slave market at New Orleans. These wretched people are to be sold singly, or in lots, to suit purchasers. They are food for the cotton-field and the deadly sugar-mill. Mark the sad procession, as it moves wearily along, and the inhuman wretch who drives them. Hear his savage yells and his blood-curdling oaths, as he hurries on his affrighted captives! There, see the old man with locks thinned and gray. Cast one glance, if you please, upon that young mother, whose shoulders are bare to the scorching sun, her briny tears falling on the brow of the babe in her arms. See, too, that girl of thirteen, weeping, yes! weeping, as she thinks of the mother from whom she has been torn! The drove moves tardily. Heat and sorrow have nearly consumed their strength; suddenly you hear a quick snap, like the discharge of a rifle; the fetters clank, and the chain rattles simultaneously; your ears are saluted with a scream, that seems to have torn its way to the centre of your soul. The crack you heard was the sound of the slave-whip; the scream you heard was from the woman you saw with the babe. Her speed had faltered under the weight of her child and her chains: that gash on her shoulder tells her to move on. Follow this drove to New Orleans. Attend the auction; see men examined like horses; see the forms of women rudely and brutally exposed to the shocking gaze of American slave-buyers. See this drove sold and separated forever; and never forget the deep, sad sobs that arose from that scattered multitude. Tell me, citizens, where, under the sun, you can witness a spectacle more fiendish and shocking. Yet this is but a glance at the American slave-trade, as it exists, at this moment, in the ruling part of the United States. . . .

Americans! your republican politics, not less than your republican religion, are flagrantly inconsistent. You boast of your love of liberty, your superior civilization, and your pure Christianity, while the whole political power of the nation (as embodied in the two great political parties) is solemnly pledged to support and perpetuate the enslavement of three millions of your countrymen. You hurl your anathemas at the crowned headed tyrants of Russia and Austria and pride yourselves on your Democratic institutions, while you yourselves consent to be the mere tools and body-guards of the tyrants of Virginia and Carolina. You invite to your shores fugitives of oppression from abroad, honor them with banquets, greet them with ovations, cheer them, toast them, salute them, protect them, and pour out your money to them like water; but the fugitives from oppression in your own land you advertise, hunt, arrest, shoot, and kill. You glory in your refinement and your universal education; yet you maintain a system as barbarous and dreadful as ever stained the character of a nation—a system begun in avarice, supported in pride, and perpetuated in cruelty. . . .

Fellow-citizens, I will not enlarge further on your national inconsistencies. The existence of slavery in this country brands your republicanism as a sham, your humanity as a base pretense, and your Christianity as a lie. It destroys your moral power abroad: it corrupts your politicians at home. It saps the foundation of religion; it makes your name a hissing and a bye-word to a mocking earth. It is the antagonistic force in your government, the only thing that seriously disturbs and endangers your Union. It fetters your progress; it is the enemy of improvement; the deadly foe of education; it fosters pride; it breeds insolence; it promotes vice; it shelters crime; it is a curse to the earth that supports it; and yet you cling to it as if it were the sheet anchor of all your hopes. Oh! be warned! be warned! a horrible reptile is coiled up in your nation's bosom; the venomous creature is nursing at the tender breast of your youthful republic; for the love of God, tear away, and fling from you the hideous monster, and let the weight of twenty millions crush and destroy it forever! ★

AUTHOR

Frederick Douglass (1817–1895) was born on a Maryland plantation to an enslaved mother and a white man rumored to be his slave master father. Douglass managed to learn to read (illegal for slaves), and used his wits and daring to escape in 1838 to New York and later New Bedford, where he worked caulking whaling ships. A brilliant writer and orator, the charismatic Douglass evolved into a leading spokesman for the abolitionist movement. Unlike many of his allies, Douglass favored equal rights for women as well as for blacks. Douglass became a regular correspondent with President Abraham Lincoln, first as a vocal critic, later as a consultant, and finally as an admirer who eulogized Lincoln after his assassination. Douglass continued speaking and publishing after the war, and went on to become the American consul general to Haiti (1889–1891).

RESPONSE

Slavery was the single most important political issue in the 1850s, and Douglass's words and actions helped to inspire outrage against it, unite people in opposition to it, and cause its downfall. Douglass's leadership helped influence President Lincoln to take a stronger stand against slavery—initially Lincoln had favored only preventing slavery's spread from the states in which it already existed. And he helped convince Lincoln to allow former slaves to serve as soldiers in the Union Army, which helped hasten the end of the war in the Union's favor.

Gordon was a slave who escaped from a Louisiana plantation in 1863. He fled to a Union Army base, where his scars from brutal whippings were revealed during a medical exam and photographed. The image became famous, helping wake up all Americans to the horrors of slavery. Gordon later joined the Union Army and fought at the Siege of Port Hudson.

A novel that inspired the abolitionist cause

The novel *Uncle Tom's Cabin* (1852) was the most popular piece of anti-slavery writing before the Civil War, selling more than 300,000 copies in its first year of publication. Harriet Beecher Stowe, a white woman, was the author. The novel told the story of Uncle Tom, a black slave, who was harshly treated by Simon Legree, a cruel white overseer. Stowe's novel became a rallying cry for abolitionists, but it outraged slave owners, who believed her depiction of slavery to be unfair.

Upon meeting Stowe in 1853, President Abraham Lincoln remarked, "So you're the little woman who made this great war?"

THE EMANCIPATION PROCLAMATION

ABRAHAM LINCOLN

January 1, 1863

On July 22, 1862, President Abraham Lincoln read to his cabinet a draft of an emancipation proclamation. Secretary of State William Seward suggested that Lincoln wait until the North had won a military victory in the Civil War to announce it. The northern triumph at the Battle of Antietam on September 17, 1862, provided Lincoln with his chance. Several days later he made public the preliminary Emancipation Proclamation, which gave Confederate states until January 1, 1863, to rejoin the Union. After that, all slaves in states still in rebellion against the Union would be freed.

Up to this point, Lincoln had fought against the expansion of slavery into territories that were not yet states, like Kansas and Nebraska. Though he morally opposed slavery, he was willing to allow it to remain where it already existed, at least for a time, in order to preserve the Union.

The Southern states refused to rejoin the Union. So, true to his word, Lincoln issued the Emancipation Proclamation on New Year's Day in 1863, ordering that slaves held in the Confederate states "shall be then, thenceforward, and forever free." The Emancipation Proclamation signaled the beginning of the end of slavery in the United States and opened the door to full citizenship for African-Americans.

THE EMANCIPATION PROCLAMATION

Whereas on the 22nd day of September, A.D. 1862, a proclamation was issued by the President of the United States, containing, among other things, the following, to wit:

That on the 1st day of January, A.D. 1863, all persons held as slaves within any State or designated part of a State the people whereof shall then be in rebellion against the United States shall be then, thenceforward, and forever free; and the executive government of the United States, including the military and naval authority thereof, will recognize and maintain the freedom of such persons and will do no act or acts to repress such persons, or any of them, in any efforts they may make for their actual freedom.

That the executive will on the 1st day of January aforesaid, by proclamation, designate the States and parts of States, if any, in which the people thereof, respectively, shall then be in rebellion against the United States; and the fact that any State or the people thereof shall on that day be in good faith represented in the Congress of the United States by members chosen thereto at elections wherein a majority of the qualified voters of such States shall have participated shall, in the absence of strong countervailing testimony, be deemed conclusive evidence that such State and the people thereof are not then in rebellion against the United States.

Now, therefore, I, Abraham Lincoln, President of the United States, by virtue of the power in me vested as Commander-in-Chief of the Army and Navy of the United States in time of actual armed rebellion against the authority and government of the United States, and as a fit and necessary war measure for suppressing said rebellion, do, on this 1st day of January, A.D. 1863, and in accordance with my purpose so to do, publicly proclaimed for the full period of one hundred days from the first day above mentioned, order and designate as the States and parts of States wherein the people thereof, respectively, are this day in rebellion against the United States the following, to wit:

Arkansas, Texas, Louisiana (except the parishes of St. Bernard, Plaquemines, Jefferson, St. John, St. Charles, St. James, Ascension, Assumption, Terrebonne, Lafourche, St. Mary, St. Martin, and Orleans, including the city of New Orleans), Mississippi. Alabama, Florida, Georgia, South Carolina, North Carolina, and Virginia (except the forty-eight counties

►——→

designated as West Virginia, and also the counties of Berkeley, Accomac, Northampton, Elizabeth City, York, Princess Anne, and Norfolk, including the cities of Norfolk and Portsmouth), and which excepted parts are for the present left precisely as if this proclamation were not issued.

And by virtue of the power and for the purpose aforesaid, I do order and declare that all persons held as slaves within said designated States and parts of States are, and henceforth shall be, free: and that the Executive Government of the United States, including the military and naval authorities thereof, will recognize and maintain the freedom of said persons.

And I hereby enjoin upon the people so declared to be free to abstain from all violence, unless in necessary self-defense; and I recommend to them that, in all causes when allowed, they labor faithfully for reasonable wages.

And I further declare and make known that such persons of suitable condition will be received into the armed service of the United States to garrison forts, positions, stations, and other places, and to man vessels of all sorts in said service.

And upon this act, sincerely believed to be an act of justice, warranted by the Constitution upon military necessity, I invoke the considerate judgment of mankind and the gracious favor of Almighty God. ★

Word of the proclamation

spread quickly to Southern slaves. They knew that their freedom was at hand. When they saw the Northern armies coming, many simply stole away to the Union side or refused to work for their masters. By the end of the war, one Union soldier in eight was African-American.

Before signing

the Emancipation Proclamation, President Lincoln said, "I never, in my life, felt more certain that I was doing right than I do in signing this paper."

A Union soldier reads the Emancipation Proclamation by torchlight to newly freed slaves in this idealized illustration.

Many antislavery groups thought President Lincoln should have freed the slaves in all the states. It is estimated that of the nation's four million slaves, about 830,000 were not freed by the provisions of the proclamation. It did not apply to the four slave states loyal to the Union (Delaware, Kentucky, Maryland, and Missouri) and did not affect slaves in Southern and Western territory held by Union forces.

Lincoln reads the Emancipation Proclamation to members of his cabinet.

The Emancipation Proclamation affected only states that had seceded from the Union. The four slave states loyal to the Union were exempted.

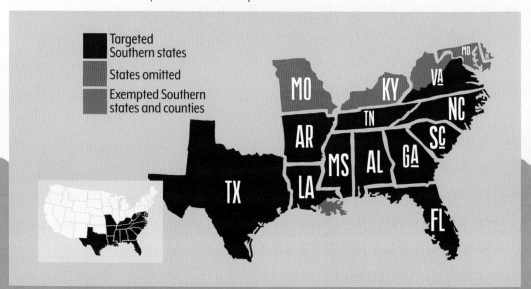

Targeted Southern states

States omitted

Exempted Southern states and counties

MO KY VA MD AR TN NC MS AL GA SC TX LA FL

AUTHOR

Abraham Lincoln (1809–1865) was the sixteenth president of the United States. He won the Republican nomination and then the presidential election in 1860, mainly because he was considered a moderate on the slavery issue. During the first year of the war, Lincoln sought only to prevent the spread of slavery into new territories, not to end it. Though he personally hated slavery, he desperately wanted to keep the Union together. As the war continued, Lincoln became more confident in taking an antislavery position.

RESPONSE

Enslaved and free blacks, abolitionists, and other opponents of slavery were overjoyed. In the North, members of Lincoln's Republican party tended to support the document, while the opposing Democratic party criticized it out of fear of the potential power of free blacks. Many Southerners attacked the proclamation, saying that Lincoln was a dictator who had overstepped his authority. Many feared it would cause slaves to rebel. By making the elimination of slavery a goal of the Union, Lincoln blocked the European powers from aiding the Confederacy, since most of them had already outlawed slavery. The bravery of African-American soldiers solidified Northern opposition to slavery, especially among Union fighters.

Lincoln's original handwritten version of the Emancipation Proclamation belonged to his son and was destroyed in the terrible Chicago Fire of 1871, but it had been photographed earlier.

One month before he issued the proclamation, President Lincoln wrote in a letter, "My paramount object in this struggle is to save the Union and is not either to save or to destroy slavery. If I could save the Union without freeing any slave, I would do it; and if I could do it by freeing all the slaves, I would do it; and if I could save it by freeing some and leaving others alone, I would also do that."

Frederick Douglass, one of the most important African-American leaders in the nineteenth century, said, "I took the proclamation for a little more than it purported and saw in its spirit a life and power far beyond its letter."

THE GETTYSBURG ADDRESS

ABRAHAM LINCOLN

November 19, 1863

In November, a new national cemetery was dedicated at Gettysburg, Pennsylvania. The Union Army had won a great Civil War victory there three months earlier. About 50,000 soldiers had been killed or wounded at the Battle of Gettysburg in just three days of fighting, making it one of the bloodiest battles in history. The famous orator Edward Everett was the main speaker at the dedication. He spoke for nearly two hours. Then President Abraham Lincoln stood up. He spoke for about two minutes. His ten-sentence address contains fewer than 300 words. In simple language Lincoln remembered those who had died in the battle and reminded soldiers and civilians alike why they were fighting the war.

The Gettysburg Address is one of the most moving tributes ever made to those who died in war and to the ideals that led them to sacrifice their lives.

THE GETTYSBURG ADDRESS

Four score and seven years ago our fathers brought forth on this continent, a new nation, conceived in liberty, and dedicated to the proposition that all men are created equal.

Now we are engaged in a great civil war, testing whether that nation or any nation so conceived and so dedicated, can long endure. We are met on a great battle-field of that war. We have come to dedicate a portion of that field, as a final resting place for those who here gave their lives that that nation might live. It is altogether fitting and proper that we should do this.

But, in a larger sense, we can not dedicate—we can not consecrate—we can not hallow—this ground. The brave men, living and dead, who struggled here, have consecrated it, far above our poor power to add or detract. The world will little note, nor long remember what we say here, but it can never forget what they did here. It is for us the living, rather, to be dedicated here to the unfinished work which they who fought here have thus far so nobly advanced. It is rather for us to be here dedicated to the great task remaining before us—that from these honored dead we take increased devotion to that cause for which they gave the last full measure of devotion—that we here highly resolve that these dead shall not have died in vain—that this nation, under God, shall have a new birth of freedom—and that government of the people, by the people, for the people, shall not perish from the earth. ★

Lincoln was invited to speak at Gettysburg only a few weeks before the ceremony. Because everyone expected great things from the main speaker, Edward Everett, Lincoln was asked merely to make "a few appropriate remarks." The audience gathered for the ceremony included ordinary citizens as well as famous figures.

This is a photograph of Civil War private Francis E. Brownell, 11th New York Infantry: One Union officer said about the Battle of Gettysburg, "I tried to ride over the field but could not, for dead and wounded lay too thick to guide a horse through them."

Many writers have reported that Lincoln wrote the address on the back of an envelope while riding on the train to Gettysburg. This story is not true. He planned the speech in advance and drafted several different versions. The "final" copy, handwritten by Lincoln for publication in 1864, differed a little from the speech he gave (there were no audio recordings at the time). This final version is the only copy Lincoln signed.

AUTHOR

Lincoln was tall and awkward-looking, from a poor frontier family, and nearly completely self-educated. He was funny and loved to tell stories, and he was frequently underestimated by allies and opponents alike. But he was whip-smart, and proved to be a shrewd commander-in-chief of the Union armies and a master at resolving political disputes. These qualities helped him win reelection in 1864. Abraham Lincoln is judged by many as the greatest American president, having effectively ended slavery and guided the Union to victory in the Civil War.

RESPONSE

The audience responded to Lincoln's speech by clapping politely. Lincoln felt his "little speech" was "a flat failure." Southern newspapers attacked the address, and many northern papers praised it. *Harpers Weekly* magazine said that Lincoln spoke "from the heart to the heart."

Five different drafts of the Address exist. Most Lincoln experts consider the 272-word Bliss version of the text, handwritten by Lincoln after the address for publication, to be the final text.

Lincoln held his second version as he spoke, but he made some changes during the address. One was to add the phrase "under God" to the last sentence.

THE FOURTEENTH AMENDMENT

July 9, 1868

After the Civil War, the Republican majority in Congress pushed through the Fourteenth Amendment. Without actually using the word "slave" or "slavery," the amendment expanded the definition of American citizenship to include all former slaves. It also declared that the states could not enact or enforce any laws that would deny citizens their rights and privileges, and it extended the same legal protections that white citizens had against being arrested and detained, or otherwise deprived of their "life, liberty, and property." The amendment is the first national document that granted major rights to the newly freed slaves.

THE FOURTEENTH AMENDMENT

Section 1. All persons born or naturalized in the United States, and subject to the jurisdiction thereof, are citizens of the United States and of the State wherein they reside. No State shall make or enforce any law which shall abridge the privileges or immunities of citizens of the United States; nor shall any State deprive any person of life, liberty, or property, without due process of law: nor deny to any person within its jurisdiction the equal protection of the laws.

Section 2. Representatives shall be apportioned among the several States according to their respective numbers, counting the whole number of persons in each State, excluding Indians not taxed. But when the right to vote at any election for the choice of electors for President and Vice President of the United States, Representatives in Congress, the Executive and Judicial officers of a State, or the members of the Legislature thereof, is denied to any of the male inhabitants of such State, being twenty-one years of age, and citizens of the United States, or in any way abridged, except for participating in rebellion, or other crime, the basis of representation therein shall be reduced in the proportion which the number of such male citizens shall bear to the whole number of male citizens twenty-one years of age in such State.

Section 3. No person shall be a Senator or Representative in Congress, or elector of President and Vice President, or hold any office, civil or military, under the United States, or under any State, who, having previously taken an oath, as a member of Congress, or as an officer of the United States, or as a member of any State legislature, or as an executive or judicial officer of any State, to support the Constitution of the United States, shall have engaged in insurrection or rebellion against the same, or given aid or comfort to the enemies thereof. But Congress may by a vote of two-thirds of each House, remove such disability.

Section 4. The validity of the public debt of the United States, authorized by law, including debts incurred for payment of pensions and bounties for services in suppressing insurrection or rebellion, shall not be questioned. But neither the United States nor any State shall assume or pay any debt or obligation incurred in aid of insurrection or rebellion against the United States, or any claim for the loss or emancipation of any slave; but all such debts, obligations, and claims shall be held illegal and void.

Section 5. The Congress shall have the power to enforce, by appropriate legislation, the provisions of this article. ★

After the war, Congress passed the Fourteenth Amendment, making African-Americans citizens and guaranteeing all citizens "the equal protection of the laws." But living conditions for black citizens lagged far behind their new protection under the law.

The Fourteenth Amendment did not specifically prohibit segregation. Also, a state might choose to prevent African-Americans from voting, but there was a penalty: the state's representation in Congress would be reduced.

After the Civil War, many former slaves found themselves homeless and few had the skills necessary to build an independent life. The U.S. War Department established the Freedmen's Bureau in 1865 for the purpose of providing medical, educational, and financial assistance for the millions of impoverished southern African-Americans.

President Johnson (1808–1875) opposed the extension of civil rights and suffrage to black Southerners—and, not surprisingly, he opposed the amendment. He made it the main issue of the 1866 congressional elections. But most Northerners had come to believe that African-Americans should have the rights of citizens. Therefore, voters elected a large majority of Republicans who supported the amendment, which Congress passed in June 1866.

The amendment also increased the power of the national government, while decreasing the power of the states. Now the federal government had the responsibility for guaranteeing all Americans their equal rights under the law.

In July 1867, President Johnson asked Frederick Douglass to take charge of the Freedmen's Bureau. This was the first major government post offered to an African-American. Douglass considered the request but then refused the position. He did not want to help Johnson, a man whose policies and beliefs he hated.

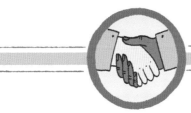

RESPONSE

By February 1867 nearly every Southern and border state had rejected the Fourteenth Amendment. Republican radicals in Congress decided to pressure these states to support the amendment by making their readmission to the Union (after they had seceded and waged the Civil War) depend on their ratifying it. This strategy eventually worked, and seven Southern states passed it in 1868. Enough states had now passed the amendment to make it the law of the land.

Frederick Douglass (see p. 80) was a crusader in the fight to end slavery and was recognized as one of America's first great black writers and speakers. During the Civil War he served as an adviser to Abraham Lincoln, and later fought for the adoption of the Fourteenth Amendment. He realized that the struggle was not over when slavery ended and said, "Slavery is not abolished until the black man has the ballot."

President Lincoln's successor, Andrew Johnson, was a Southerner who had remained loyal to the Union during the war. He believed it was up to the states, and not the federal government, to determine their own laws governing the rights of African-Americans.

VOTE HERE

FIFTEENTH AMENDMENT

February 3, 1870

By passing the Fifteenth Amendment, Republicans in Congress hoped to fulfill their promise of equality to African-Americans in the aftermath of the Civil War. The amendment gave African-American males the vote.

The amendment opened the way for participation in the political process, and thousands of black citizens voted for the first time. But as time passed, blacks were sometimes prevented from voting by cities and states that imposed purposely tricky literacy tests and other obstacles to voting. African-Americans have fought against continued oppression, forming organizations such as the National Association for the Advancement of Colored People (NAACP)

in 1909. During the following century, leaders such as W. E. B. Du Bois, A. Philip Randolph, John Lewis, Martin Luther King, Jr., and Malcolm X led the struggle for equality. Their work, together with that of political leaders such as John and Robert Kennedy and Lyndon Johnson, resulted in the Voting Rights Act of 1965. The act ensured that African-Americans and those of other ethnicities could freely exercise their right to vote. After the election of the nation's first African-American president, Barack Obama, in 2008, twenty states passed laws requiring voters to show photo IDs or put other restrictions on the right to vote—laws that many believe are designed to suppress turnout among minority voters.

THE FIFTEENTH AMENDMENT

Section 1. The right of citizens of the United States to vote shall not be denied or abridged by the United States or any State on account of race, color, or previous condition of servitude.

Section 2. The Congress shall have power to enforce this article by appropriate legislation. ★

RESPONSE

Most Southern states had to pass the amendment because of pressure from the national government, and the amendment became law in February 1870. African-Americans in the South began voting soon afterward. By late 1870, all the former Confederate states had been readmitted to the Union, and most were controlled by the Republican Party, thanks in large part to the support of black voters. During the 1880s, African-Americans were elected to political office throughout the South. However, in the 1890s, Southern states began adding literacy tests and using other tactics that ended nearly all African-American voting in the South. Southern African-Americans only began to vote again when the modern civil rights movement successfully began to challenge these tactics in the 1960s.

This illustration entitled *The First Vote* appeared in the popular magazine *Harpers Weekly* in 1867. The men standing in line to vote represent the various professions of African-Americans: a worker with his tools, a well-dressed middle-class man, and a Union soldier.

An illustration by the famous artists Currier and Ives features the first African-American senators and representatives in the 41st and 42nd Congress. All were elected from Southern states. Senator Hiram Revels (left) was elected in 1870 to the seat that had been occupied by Jefferson Davis (the president of the Confederacy) when the South left the Union before the Civil War.

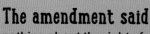

The amendment said nothing about the right of African-American women to vote. This was not surprising—because no women had the right to vote until the Nineteenth Amendment was ratified in 1920 (see p. 124).

I WILL FIGHT NO MORE FOREVER

CHIEF JOSEPH

October 5, 1877

In 1877 white settlers in Oregon wanted to take the lands of the Nez Perce Indians. The government responded to the settlers' land hunger by ordering the Nez Perce to remove themselves to a small reservation in Idaho. The Nez Perce refused, and war broke out between the tribe and the U.S. Army. After defeating the army in their first encounter, the Nez Perce realized that they would soon be hunted down. Therefore, they decided to flee to Canada. The trek was 1,300 miles. U.S. troops pursued the band of almost 600 Indians every step of the way, but the Nez Perce managed to evade them for nearly 75 days. Then, close to the Canadian border, the Nez Perce were trapped. His band surrounded, the Nez Perce leader, Chief Joseph, was forced to surrender to the army.

Chief Joseph's speech is one of the most famous Native American documents. Probably no other Native American voice so powerfully describes the tragedy of Indian displacement and defeat. Chief Joseph's surrender in 1877 nearly marked the end of the Indian wars. No other big battle occurred until the last, the Wounded Knee Massacre, in 1890.

I WILL FIGHT NO MORE FOREVER

Tell General Howard I know his heart. What he told me before I have in my heart. I am tired of fighting. Our chiefs are killed. Looking Glass is dead. Too-hul-hul-sote is dead. The old men are all dead. It is the young men who say yes or no. He who led on the young men is dead. It is cold and we have no blankets. The little children are freezing to death. My people, some of them, have run away to the hills, and have no blankets, no food; no one knows where they are— perhaps freezing to death. I want to have time to look for my children and see how many of them I can find. Maybe I shall find them among the dead. Hear me, my chiefs. I am tired; my heart is sick and sad. From where the sun now stands I will fight no more forever. ★

This photograph is of Nez Perce Chief Joseph. He once said, "We only ask an even chance to live as other men live. We ask to be recognized as men. We ask that the same law shall work alike on all men."

AUTHOR

Chief Joseph (c. 1840–1904), whose Indian name meant "Thunder Rolling Down the Mountain," was a great Native American warrior and leader. He was one of the first of his tribe to convert to Christianity, and favored peace with the white man. The U.S. commander had promised Joseph that he would be allowed to return to his homeland, but after his surrender, the federal government sent him and the surviving members of his tribe to the Indian Territory in present-day Oklahoma. There, most of the trek's survivors died of disease and starvation. Around 1885 Chief Joseph was moved to the Colville Indian Reservation in Washington, where he died in 1904.

RESPONSE

Many white Americans were moved by the bravery of the Nez Perce during their retreat. Even the commanding officers to whom Chief Joseph surrendered felt sympathetic to him and were impressed with his strategy and tactics during the retreat. Unsurprisingly, any local whites were happy to possess the Indians' lands.

Chief Joseph's doctor attributed the warrior's death to a "broken heart."

In his speech Chief Joseph spoke of the death of "He who led on the young men." This was Ollokot, his younger brother.

Before the government tried to force them onto a reservation, the Nez Perce were a peaceful tribe. They bred livestock, and their many horses and cattle grazed in the rich meadows on their lands.

Looking Glass was a Nez Perce warrior. He advised Chief Joseph against trying to make the dangerous escape attempt from Montana to Canada. Looking Glass was killed during the retreat by a scout hired by the U.S. Army.

STATEMENT ON THE CAUSES OF WOUNDED KNEE

CHIEF RED CLOUD

1890

As Native Americans were pushed by white settlers off their lands and onto reservations, fears of an Indian uprising increased dramatically during the administration of President Benjamin Harrison. He ordered U.S. troops to areas near reservations, including that of the Oglala Lakota Sioux in South Dakota. Some of the Lakota Sioux had recently begun following Wovoka, a Nevada Paiute who claimed that on Judgment Day an Indian Messiah would restore the lands that the Indians had lost to white Americans, who would then disappear. Wovoka's followers performed the Ghost Dance ceremony to make Judgment Day come sooner, which alarmed local whites as it became more popular. Tensions increased between whites and the Indians.

Fearing that the white soldiers might massacre them, some three hundred Sioux fled the reservation. On December 29, 1890, the U.S. Army surrounded the Sioux at Wounded Knee Creek in South Dakota. The Indians raised a surrender flag. But a shot fired, possibly in a struggle over a surrendered weapon, caused the troops to begin shooting to kill. In minutes, at least 150 Lakota Sioux lay dying, including women and children. In this document, the Sioux warrior and Chief Red Cloud describes the events leading up to the massacre.

STATEMENT OF THE CAUSES OF WOUNDED KNEE

I will tell you the reason for the trouble. When we first made treaties with the Government, our old life and our old customs were about to end: the game on which we lived was disappearing; the whites were closing around us, and nothing remained for us but to adopt their ways,—the Government promised us all the means necessary to make our living out of the land, and to instruct us how to do it, and with abundant food to support us until we could take care of ourselves. We looked forward with hope to the time we could be as independent as the whites, and have a voice in the Government.

The army officers could have helped better than anyone else but we were not left to them. An Indian Department was made with a large number of agents and other officials drawing large salaries— then came the beginning of trouble; these men took care of themselves but not of us. It was very hard to deal with the government through them—they could make more for themselves by keeping us back than by helping us forward.

We did not get the means for working our lands; the few things they gave us did little good.

Our rations began to be reduced; they said we were lazy. That is false. How does any man of sense suppose that so great a number of people could get work at once unless they were at once supplied with the means to work and instructors enough to teach them?

Our ponies were taken away from us under the promise that they would be replaced by oxen and large horses; it was long before we saw any, and then we got very few. We tried with the means we had, but on one pretext or another, we were shifted from one place to another, or were told that such a transfer was coming. Great efforts were made to break up our customs, but nothing was done to introduce us to customs of the whites. Everything was done to break up the power of the real chiefs.

Those old men really wished their people to improve, but little men, so-called chiefs, were made to act as disturbers and agitators. Spotted Tail wanted the ways of the whites, but an assassin was found to remove him. This was charged to the Indians because an Indian did it, but who set on the Indian? I was abused and slandered, to weaken my influence for good. This was done by men paid by the government to teach us the ways of the whites. I have visited many other tribes and found that the same things were done amongst them: all was done to discourage us and nothing to encourage us. I saw men paid by the government to help us, all very busy making money for themselves, but doing nothing for us. . . .

STATEMENT OF THE CAUSES OF WOUNDED KNEE **103**

The men who counted (census) told all around that we were feasting and wasting food. Where did he see it? How could we waste what we did not have? We felt we were mocked in our misery; we had no newspaper and no one to speak for us. Our rations were again reduced.

You who eat three times a day and see your children well and happy around you cannot understand what a starving Indian feels! We were faint with hunger and maddened by despair. We held our dying children and felt their little bodies tremble as their soul went out and left only a dead weight in our hands. They were not very heavy but we were faint and the dead weighed us down. There was no hope on earth. God seemed to have forgotten.

Some one had been talking of the Son of God and said He had come. The people did not know; they did not care; they snatched at hope; they screamed like crazy people to Him for mercy; they caught at the promise they heard He had made.

The white people were frightened and called for soldiers. We begged for life and the white men thought we wanted theirs; we heard the soldiers were coming. We did not fear. We hoped we could tell them our suffering and could get help. The white men told us the soldiers meant to kill us: we did not believe it but some were frightened and ran away to the Bad Lands. The soldiers came. They said: "don't be afraid—we come to make peace, not war." It was true; they bought us food. But the hunger-crazed who had taken fright at the soldiers' coining and went to the Bad Lands could not be induced to return to the horrors of reservation life. They were called Hostiles and the Government sent the army to force them back to their reservation prison. ★

According to the Ghost Dance religion, which combined messianic Christianity with Native American traditions, if believers lived righteous lives and performed the Ghost Dance ritual, the white invaders would vanish, the bison would come back, the living would be reunited with the dead, and the old ways would return.

Bodies littered the battleground at Wounded Knee. One Native American later recalled the battle: "I can see that something else died there in the bloody mud, and was buried in the blizzard. A people's dream died there."

Black Elk, a survivor of Wounded Knee, later said, "A terrible blizzard raged for two days covering the bodies with Nature's great white blanket; some lay in piles of four or five; others in twos or threes or singly, where they fell until the storm subsided."

Big Foot's Minniconjou band was photographed at the Ghost Dance on the Cheyenne River on August 9, 1890. Four months later, nearly all were killed. The U.S. Army surrounded the Sioux at Wounded Knee Creek and turned their guns on them.

Just a few months before the massacre at Wounded Knee, the federal government appointed a new agent to manage Native American affairs in the region. The agent, Daniel Royer, a political appointee, was inexperienced and fearful of Native Americans. Royer believed that the Ghost Dance was a war dance, and immediately began sending warnings to Washington urging that troops be sent to protect citizens from war.

AUTHOR

Red Cloud (1822–1909) was a great Sioux chief and warrior. Throughout the 1860s, he led the Sioux in a fight to keep white settlers out of Sioux lands in present-day South Dakota, Montana, and Wyoming. This struggle has been called Red Cloud's War. By 1868, the army was forced to give up three forts it had built in the region, and the government promised not to construct any roads through Sioux lands. The victory was short-lived, however. By the middle of the next decade, war had returned to the region.

RESPONSE

The army had responded to the fears of settlers and government officials, who were relieved and happy at being able to use land that had belonged to the Sioux without having to worry about being attacked by them. Those Sioux who had not been at Wounded Knee were filled with sadness. The tribe's Ghost Dance rites and rituals ended. The Wounded Knee Massacre ended the military warfare between the western Indians and whites, and Native Americans were largely confined to federal reservations thereafter.

Chief Red Cloud poses with his son and granddaughter. At the time of this photograph, Red Cloud was ninety years old.

The Ghost Dance chant begins: "The whole world is coming. / A nation is coming, a nation is coming. / The Eagle has brought the message to the tribe."

After they killed the Sioux warriors, the soldiers shot the Indian women and children who were attempting to run away from the battlefield.

TWENTY YEARS AT HULL-HOUSE

JANE ADDAMS

1910

I n 1860, 20 percent of the American population lived in cities. By the late 1890s, that number had nearly doubled, thanks to an influx of immigrants, many of them poor and uneducated.

As a result, increasing numbers of American reformers focused on helping the urban poor. The reformers organized community centers in slum areas, where many immigrants lived. One such reformer was Jane Addams. In 1889 Addams and her college friend Ellen Starr founded Hull-House on Halsted Street, in one of Chicago's worst slums. Hull-House was a "settlement house" whose mission was to help immigrants transition into productive lives and jobs by teaching them middle-class American values. Addams

and the other settlement workers lived in Hull-House, offering neighborhood people services, guidance, and even food and baths. It grew to have a nursery, a kindergarten, a gymnasium, and a playground, and offered activities such as music and art classes.

By 1900 about 100 settlement houses had been established across the country. Hull-House served as a model for many of them. Addams's work caused many Americans to support the need for social reform. Today, largely because of her efforts, community centers and settlement houses exist in cities across the United States. In 1910 she wrote about her experiences as a reformer in *Twenty Years at Hull-House*. The following passage is from chapter 5, "First Days at Hull-House."

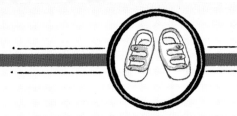

TWENTY YEARS AT HULL-HOUSE, AN EXCERPT

. . . The dozens of younger children who from the first came to Hull-House were organized into groups which were not quite classes and not quite clubs. The values of these groups consisted almost entirely in arousing a higher imagination and in giving the children the opportunity which they could not have in the crowded schools, for initiative and for independent social relationships. The public schools then contained little hand work of any sort, so that naturally any instruction which we provided for the children took the direction of this supplementary work. But it required a constant effort that the pressure of poverty itself should not defeat the educational aim. The Italian girls in the sewing classes would count that day lost when they could not carry home a garment, and the insistence that it should be neatly made seemed a super-refinement to those in dire need of clothing.

As these clubs have been continued during the twenty years they have developed classes in the many forms of handicraft which the newer education is so rapidly adapting for the delight of children: but they still keep their essentially social character and still minister to that large number of children who leave school the very week they are fourteen years old, only too eager to close the schoolroom door forever on a tiresome task that is at last well over. It seems to us important that these children shall find themselves permanently attached to a House that offers them evening clubs and classes with their old companions, that merges as easily as possible the school life into the working life and does what it can to find places for the bewildered young things looking for work. A large proportion of the delinquent boys brought into the juvenile court in Chicago are the oldest sons in large families whose wages are needed at home. The grades from which many of them leave school, as the records show, are piteously far from the seventh and eighth where the very first instruction in manual training [course of training to develop skill in using the hands and to teach practical arts such as woodworking and metalworking] is given, nor have they been caught by any other abiding interest. . . .

In those early days we were often asked why we had come to live on Halsted Street when we could afford to live somewhere else. I remember one man who used to shake his head and say it was "the strangest thing he had met in his experience," but who was finally convinced that it was "not strange but natural." In time it came to seem natural to all of us

➤

that the Settlement should be there. It is natural to feed the hungry and care for the sick, it is certainly natural to give pleasure to the young, comfort to the aged, and to minister to the deep-seated craving for social intercourse that all men feel. Whoever does it is reward-ed by something which, if not gratitude, is at least spontaneous and vital and lacks that irksome sense of obligation with which a substantial benefit is too often acknowledged.

In addition to the neighbors who responded to the receptions and classes, we found those who were too battered and oppressed to care for them. To these, however, was left that susceptibility to the bare offices [acts] of humanity which raises such offices into a bond of fellowship.

From the first it seemed understood that we were ready to perform the humblest neigh-borhood services. We were asked to wash the newborn babies, and to prepare the dead for burial, to nurse the sick, and to "'mind the children. . . .'"

We were also early impressed with the curious isolation of many of the immigrants; an Italian woman once expressed her pleasure in the red roses that she saw at one of our receptions in surprise that they had been "brought so fresh all the way from Italy." She would not believe for an instant that they had been grown in America. She said that she had lived in Chicago for six years and had never seen any roses, whereas in Italy she had seen them every summer in great profusion. During all that time, of course, the woman had lived within ten blocks of a florists window; she had not been more than a five-cent car ride away from the public parks; but she had never dreamed of faring forth for herself, and no one had taken her. Her conception of America had been the untidy street in which she lived and had made her long struggle to adapt herself to American ways.

But in spite of some untoward experiences, we were constantly impressed with the uni-form kindness and courtesy we received. Perhaps these first days laid the simple human foundations which are certainly essential for continuous living among the poor: first, gen-uine preference for residence in an industrial quarter to any other part of the city, because it is interesting and makes the human appeal; and second, the conviction . . . that the things which make men alike are finer and better than the things that keep them apart, and that these basic likenesses, if they are properly accentuated, easily transcend the less essential differences of race, language, creed, and tradition.

Perhaps even in those first days we made a beginning toward that object which was afterward stated in our charter: "To provide a center for a higher civic and social life; to institute and maintain educational and philanthropic enterprises, and to investigate and improve the conditions in the industrial districts of Chicago."★

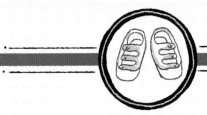

The immigrant families that Hull-House and other settlement houses served often lived in cities in overcrowded, run-down buildings called tenements. The famous photographer Jacob Riis took this photograph of an Italian immigrant family of seven living in a one-room tenement apartment around 1890.

Most settlement house workers were young women. Some had just graduated from college. One British visitor described the workers at Hull-House as "strong-minded and energetic women, bustling about their various enterprises." Another visitor said Jane Addams was "the only saint the United States has produced."

Jane Addams was only twenty-nine when she and Ellen Starr established Hull-House in an old mansion. Addams never moved from Hull-House, which expanded to include 13 buildings.

In this 1900 photo taken at Hull-House, children work together with clay, in what Jane Addams described as "not quite classes and not quite clubs," providing skills and social time for immigrants.

Hull-House stood on five-mile-long Halsted Street, which teemed with Irish, German, Russian, Italian, and Polish immigrants.

THE HULL HOUSE, CHICAGO

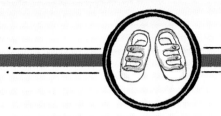

AUTHOR

Born into a prosperous Illinois family, Jane Addams (1860–1935) became interested in reform work while traveling in Europe. The example of English reformers who voluntarily lived in London slums moved her to found Hull-House. Although she remained committed to Hull-House, Addams soon realized that real reform could come about only through legislation. So she became involved in politics. She and her supporters helped to end child labor, limit the hours of working women, and set up the juvenile court system. During the last years of her life, she organized women around the world for peace. In 1931 she became the first American woman to win the Nobel Peace Prize.

RESPONSE

Jane Addams won the grateful support of people who were helped by Hull-House and her fellow reformers. Her account of Hull-House in the book excerpted here won the support of the public for her work and for the reform movement. Some critics argued that settlement houses were breeding grounds for radical politics and caused immigrants to abandon their ancestral faith—and in many cases failed to improve their lot.

While at Hull-House, Addams discovered that poor immigrant children needed to be taught more than just reading and writing. She believed that this type of education "fails to give the child any clue to the life about him."

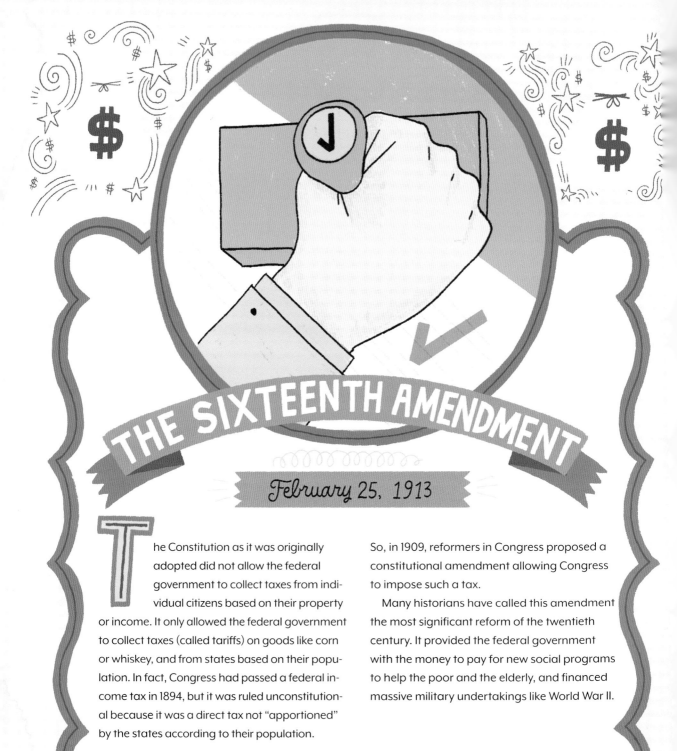

THE SIXTEENTH AMENDMENT

February 25, 1913

The Constitution as it was originally adopted did not allow the federal government to collect taxes from individual citizens based on their property or income. It only allowed the federal government to collect taxes (called tariffs) on goods like corn or whiskey, and from states based on their population. In fact, Congress had passed a federal income tax in 1894, but it was ruled unconstitutional because it was a direct tax not "apportioned" by the states according to their population.

So, in 1909, reformers in Congress proposed a constitutional amendment allowing Congress to impose such a tax.

Many historians have called this amendment the most significant reform of the twentieth century. It provided the federal government with the money to pay for new social programs to help the poor and the elderly, and financed massive military undertakings like World War II.

THE SIXTEENTH AMENDMENT

The Congress shall have power to lay and collect taxes on incomes, from whatever source derived, without apportionment among the several States, and without regard to any census or enumeration. ★

A 1934 "Wanted" poster issued by the United States Treasury the well-known gangster Dutch Schultz who was wanted by the government for violation of the federal income tax law.

In the 1860s, the huge costs of the Civil War pushed Congress to pass the first federal income tax. This Internal Revenue Service Act placed a 3 percent tax on all incomes above $800. A new bureau, the Internal Revenue Bureau, directed the collection of taxes. Congress repealed that tax in 1872.

During the 1930s the government started to use the Sixteenth Amendment to get gangsters off the streets and into jails. The government imprisoned gang leaders such as Chicago's Al Capone on charges that they evaded paying income tax on the huge amounts of money they made illegally.

In the 1920s, crowds of Americans filled out tax forms at the IRS office to get them in on time.

On July 12, 1909, Congress approved an amendment to the U.S. Constitution to permit federal tax on income. It was then ratified by the states and became law on February 3, 1913.

S. J. Res. 40.

Sixty-first Congress of the United States of America;

At the First Session,

Begun and held at the City of Washington on Monday, the fifteenth day of March, one thousand nine hundred and nine.

JOINT RESOLUTION

Proposing an amendment to the Constitution of the United States.

Resolved by the Senate and House of Representatives of the United States of America in Congress assembled (two-thirds of each House concurring therein), That the following article is proposed as an amendment to the Constitution of the United States, which, when ratified by the legislatures of three-fourths of the several States, shall be valid to all intents and purposes as a part of the Constitution:

"ARTICLE XVI. The Congress shall have power to lay and collect taxes on incomes, from whatever source derived, without apportionment among the several States, and without regard to any census or enumeration."

Speaker of the House of Representatives.

Vice-President of the United States and President of the Senate.

Attest.

RESPONSE

The idea of a personal income tax was popular especially in the rural West and South because many believed that wealthy businessmen would bear most of the tax burden. When it was first introduced, the tax code was quite simple, unlike today. Still, many conservative Republicans and wealthy individuals did not support the amendment.

In 1913, the first federal Form 1040 was one page long.

The federal income tax allows the federal government to maintain an army, build roads and bridges, operate national parks, enforce laws, fund programs like NASA, and carry out other important duties. Before the Sixteenth Amendment was passed, tariffs on goods and taxes shared with individual states were the only sources of funding.

Taxes on goods

that everyone needs, like corn or shoes, are considered "regressive," because they are the same for everyone—so they take up a higher percentage of a poor person's budget than they would for a rich person's. The federal income tax rate is highest for big earners and lowest for low-income individuals. This is called a "progressive" tax.

THE FOURTEEN POINTS

WOODROW WILSON

January 8, 1918

For three years President Woodrow Wilson kept the United States out of World War I. But in 1917 he reluctantly joined France, England, and their allies in the struggle against Germany. American intervention brought victory for the Allies and gave Wilson the opportunity to try to create a framework for establishing permanent peace among the world's nations. Early in 1918 he delivered a speech to Congress outlining a plan to make the world "fit and safe to live in." Wilson's peace plan, which had fourteen separate items, became known as the Fourteen Points. The first five points stated general principles for positive international conduct such as the prohibition of secret treaties, free navigation, and free trade between nations. Eight other points involved setting new boundaries in Europe after the war and creating several new countries. The fourteenth point called for an international association of countries, large and small, to put into action these principles and to resolve future international disputes. This became the League of Nations.

THE FOURTEEN POINTS

. . . We entered this war because violations of right had occurred which touched us to the quick and made the life of our own people impossible unless they were corrected and the world secured once for all against their recurrence. What we demand in this war, therefore, is nothing peculiar to ourselves. It is that the world be made fit and safe to live in; and particularly that it be made safe for every peace-loving nation which, like our own, wishes to live its own life, determine its own institutions, be assured of justice and fair dealing by the other peoples of the world as against force and selfish aggression. All the peoples of the world are in effect partners in this interest, and for our own part we see very clearly that unless justice be done to others it will not be done to us. The program of the world's peace, therefore, is our program; and that program, the only possible program as we see it, is this:

I. Open covenants of peace, openly arrived at, after which there shall be no private international understandings of any kind but diplomacy shall proceed always frankly and in the public view.

II. Absolute freedom of navigation upon the seas, outside territorial waters, alike in peace and in war, except as the seas may be closed in whole or in part by international action for the enforcement of international covenants.

III. The removal, so far as possible, of all economic barriers and the establishment of an equality of trade conditions among all the nations consenting to the peace and associating themselves for its maintenance.

IV. Adequate guarantees given and taken that national armaments will be reduced to the lowest point consistent with domestic safety.

V. A free, open-minded, and absolutely impartial adjustment of all colonial claims, based upon a strict observance of the principle that in determining all such questions of sovereignty the interests of the populations concerned must have equal weight with the equitable claims of the government whose title is to be determined.

➤

VI. The evacuation of all Russian territory and such a settlement of all questions affecting Russia as will secure the best and freest cooperation of the other nations of the world in obtaining for her an unhampered and unembarrassed opportunity for the independent determination of her own political development and national policy and assure her of a sincere welcome into the society of free nations under institutions of her own choosing, and, more than a welcome, assistance also of every kind that she may need and may herself desire. The treatment accorded Russia by her sister nations in the months to come will be the acid test of their good will, of their comprehension of her needs as distinguished from their own interests, and of their intelligent and unselfish sympathy.

VII. Belgium, the whole world will agree, must be evacuated and restored, without any attempt to limit the sovereignty which she enjoys in common with all other free nations. No other single act will serve as this will serve to restore confidence among the nations in the laws which they have themselves set and determined for the government of their relations with one another. Without this healing act the whole structure and validity of international law is forever impaired.

VIII. All French territory should be freed and the invaded portions restored, and the wrong done to France by Prussia in 1871 in the matter of Alsace-Lorraine, which has unsettled the peace of the world for nearly fifty years, should be righted, in order that peace may once more be made secure in the interest of all.

IX. A readjustment of the frontiers of Italy should be effected along clearly recognizable lines of nationality.

X. The peoples of Austria-Hungary, whose place among the nations we wish to see safeguarded and assured, should be accorded the freest opportunity of autonomous development.

XI. Rumania, Serbia, and Montenegro should be evacuated; occupied territories restored; Serbia accorded free and secure access to the sea; and the relations of the several Balkan states to one another determined by friendly counsel along historically established lines of allegiance and nationality; and international guarantees of the political and economic independence and territorial integrity of the several Balkan states should be entered into.

XII. The Turkish portions of the present Ottoman Empire should be assured a secure sovereignty, but the other nationalities which are now under the Turkish rule should be assured an undoubted security of life and an absolutely unmolested opportunity of autonomous development, and the

Dardanelles should be permanently opened as a free passage to the ships and commerce of all nations under international guarantees.

XIII. An independent Polish state should be erected which should include the territories inhabited by indisputably Polish populations, which should be assured a free and secure access to the sea, and whose political and economic independence and territorial integrity should be guaranteed by international covenant.

XIV. A general association of nations must be formed under specific covenants for the purpose of affording mutual guarantees of political independence and territorial integrity to great and small states alike. . . .

We have spoken now, surely, in terms too concrete to admit of any further doubt or question. An evident principle runs through the whole program I have outlined. It is the principle of justice to all peoples and nationalities, and their right to live on equal terms of liberty and safety with one another, whether they be strong or weak. Unless this principle be made its foundation no part of the structure of international justice can stand. The people of the United States could act upon no other principle; and to the vindication of this principle they are ready to devote their lives, their honor, and everything that they possess. The moral climax of this the culminating and final war for human liberty has come, and they are ready to put their own strength, their own highest purpose, their own integrity and devotion to the test. ★

Allied leaders meet with Woodrow Wilson at the Paris Peace Conference in 1919. David Lloyd George of Great Britain, Vittorio Orlando of Italy, and Georges Clémenceau of France all favored a more traditional settlement for peace. Wilson (at right) worked tirelessly for a peace outlined in his Fourteen Points.

President Woodrow Wilson was cheered as a hero during his 1919 visit to Dover, England. But at home the peace treaty that he had helped draw up was in trouble in Congress. On Wilson's return, he made as many as four speeches a day to persuade Americans to support the treaty, which established the League of Nations. He felt sure the League was necessary to prevent another world war. But he failed in his attempt, and the United States never joined the League of Nations.

Woodrow Wilson began his career as a university professor. While teaching at Bryn Mawr College, Wesleyan University, and Princeton University, he wrote nine books and more than 35 articles on politics and history. After serving as president of Princeton from 1902 to 1910, he was elected governor of New Jersey.

Premier Clemenceau of France was not enthusiastic about Wilson's plan. "God gave us the Ten Commandments and we broke them," he said. "Wilson gave us the Fourteen Points. We shall see."

Woodrow Wilson's unsuccessful attempt to keep America out of the war was personally exhausting. He lost sleep and looked pale and tired. When someone asked which side he hoped would win the war, Wilson said, "Neither."

AUTHOR

Woodrow Wilson (1856–1924) was the twenty-eighth president of the United States. Before entering politics, he served as president of Princeton University in New Jersey. In 1910 he became the Democratic governor of New Jersey. Two years later he was elected president on the Democratic ticket. At the outbreak of World War I, Wilson, who hated war, tried desperately to preserve American neutrality. But when Germany continued to attack United States ships with their submarines, he asked Congress to declare war. In October 1919 Wilson suffered a stroke at the end of a nationwide speaking tour to defend the peace treaty and the League of Nations. Although he completed his term, Wilson never fully recovered.

RESPONSE

Most of Wilson's points regarding the reconstruction of Europe were disregarded by the Allies in negotiating the 1919 Treaty of Versailles, which ended World War I. They were more interested in reestablishing control over territories they had lost and in punishing Germany.

But the negotiators at Versailles proposed what Wilson dreamed of—an international peacekeeping organization, later named the League of Nations. Nonetheless, the treaty was defeated in Congress on March 19, 1920. The United States finally signed a separate peace with Germany in July 1921.

Without the United States, the League of Nations was too weak to prevent World War II. But, as that war ended, Americans realized the necessity of a strong world peacekeeping organization to replace the League. When the United Nations met for the first time in London on January 10, 1946, the United States was a full member.

President Wilson doffs his hat to crowds in this photo taken during his tour of Europe after World War I. During the war American pilots dropped leaflets over Germany describing Wilson's Fourteen Points. The Americans hoped the German people would read these leaflets and be persuaded to end the war.

THE NINETEENTH AMENDMENT

August 18, 1920

Before the passage of the Nineteenth Amendment, American women had almost no legal, political, or social rights in most of the United States. They could not vote, own property, or gain custody of their children after a divorce. Many women realized that the only way to gain these rights was through the power of the ballot. So from the late 1860s on, women organized and petitioned state legislatures and Congress to give them the vote. Some religious suffragist leaders believed that "intemperance," or public consumption of alcohol, could be eliminated if women were give the vote.

Their efforts were met with intense opposition by both male and female antisuffragists. But this did not stop them. In 1916 suffragists picketed the White House, facing arrest and even jail. Congress finally gave in to the pressure and passed the Nineteenth Amendment in May 1919. On August 18, 1920, the "Susan B. Anthony Amendment," as it was later called, had been ratified by the necessary 36 of the 48 states and became part of the Constitution. With the Nineteenth Amendment, women finally won a voice in their government.

THE NINETEENTH AMENDMENT

Section 1. The right of citizens of the United States to vote shall not be denied or abridged by the United States or by any State on account of sex.

Section 2. Congress shall have power to enforce this article by appropriate legislation. ★

In February 1917 suffragists picketed outside the White House to persuade President Wilson to support the right of women to vote. The police arrested the picketers for "obstructing traffic," but later that year Wilson spoke out for the first time in support of women's suffrage.

In 1872, women could not vote in federal elections. But the National American Woman Suffrage Association backed Victoria Woodhull, the first woman to run for president of the United States—144 years before Hillary Clinton became the Democratic nominee for president in 2016. Woodhull, who was the candidate of a new party called the Equal Rights Party, could not vote for herself under the Constitution, and perhaps unsurprisingly, failed to win a single electoral vote.

After the Nineteenth Amendment became law, suffragist Carrie Chapman Catt said, "To get the word 'male' in effect out of the Constitution cost the women of the country fifty-two years of pauseless campaign. . . ."

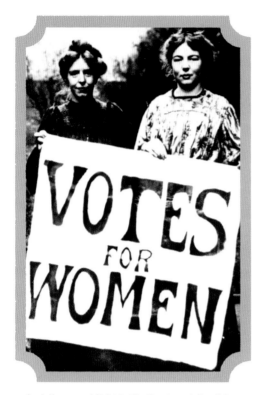

Annie Kenney and Christabel Pankhurst were influential British suffragettes who inspired many American women.

Ida B. Wells, an African-American journalist who founded the Alpha Suffrage Club of Chicago in 1913, led a group of black suffragists to the first National American Woman Suffrage Association parade in Washington, D.C. When asked to march with her group at the rear of the state's delegation so as not to offend the Southern delegates, Wells replied, "Either I go with you or not at all. I am not taking this stand because I personally wish for recognition. I am doing it for the future benefit of my whole race."

President Woodrow Wilson reversed his opposition to the Nineteenth Amendment in 1918, shifting political momentum in the nation, leading to its passage by the House of Representatives on May 21, 1919.

Two weeks later, the Senate followed suit. Tennessee became the 36th state to ratify the amendment on August 18, 1920, thereby giving the measure approval in the three-fourths of the states

necessary for an amendent to become law. Secretary of State Bainbridge Colby certified the ratification on August 26, 1920.

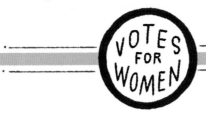

AUTHORS

Although they did not write the proposed amendment, Susan B. Anthony (1820–1906) and Carrie Chapman Catt (1859–1947) were among the most influential leaders of the American women's suffrage movement. Born to a middle-class family in Massachusetts, Susan Anthony became a teacher. Through her speeches and writing, she also roused generations of American women to the awareness that suffrage was their right. In 1900 she stepped down from the presidency of the National American Woman Suffrage Association (NAWSA). Anthony chose Carrie Chapman Catt as her successor in that position. The Wisconsin-born Catt, who, like Anthony, was a teacher, rose quickly in the suffragist movement. An excellent strategist, Catt enlisted and directed volunteers, spoke everywhere, organized events, and used the media to promote women's suffrage. Over the next 20 years, she led the movement to victory.

RESPONSE

Many activists were satisfied with what they had won. These moderates joined the recently formed League of Women Voters, whose main goal was to educate women on the issues so that they could vote intelligently. More militant suffragists felt, however, that they had not yet achieved total equality with men. In 1923 they founded the National Women's Party, which began campaigning for a constitutional Equal Rights Amendment (ERA). Congress finally passed the amendment in 1972, but only 35 of the 38 states required for ratification subsequently approved it. So, by the end of 1982, the amendment died.

Illinois, Wisconsin, and Michigan were the first states to ratify the Nineteenth Amendment, on June 10, 1919, followed by Kansas, New York, and Ohio the following week. The last states to ratify the amendment (symbolically, since the Amendment was already law) were Florida and South Carolina (1969), Georgia and Louisiana (1970), and North Carolina (1971). Mississippi became the last state to ratify the Nineteenth Amendment in 1984. Alaska and Hawaii cannot vote on the amendment as they were not yet states when Congress passed the bill.

THE IMMIGRATION ACT

May 26, 1924

From its beginnings, the United States was a land of immigrants, and took pride in considering itself as such. But in the early twentieth century, as a new wave of immigrants, mainly from southern and eastern Europe, flocked to this country, many Americans, particularly members of the labor unions, became worried that the newcomers would take away their jobs. World War I had only recently ended, and fears of ethnic violence and "un-American" customs and values multiplied—in many cases fanned by news media and politicians.

Congress responded to this pressure by passing the Immigration Act of 1924. The act limited immigration to two percent of each nationality present in the United States in the year 1890. At that time, only small numbers of eastern and southern European newcomers had entered.

The Immigration Act marked a turning point in the nation's history. For the first time, the government set broad, nation-by-nation restrictions on the number of newcomers. The act greatly reduced the number of legal immigrants while discriminating against immigrants from countries outside of northern Europe and against nonwhites. The following selection is from this act.

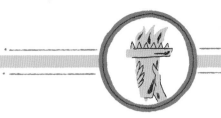

THE IMMIGRATION ACT

BY THE PRESIDENT OF THE UNITED STATES OF AMERICA A PROCLAMATION

Whereas it is provided in the act of Congress approved May 26, 1924, entitled "An act to limit the immigration of aliens into the United States, and for other purposes" that—

"The annual quota of any nationality shall be two per cent of the number of foreign-born individuals of such nationality resident in continental United States as determined by the United States census of 1890, but the minimum quota of any nationality shall be 100. . . ."

Now, therefore, I, Calvin Coolidge, President of the United States of America acting under and by virtue of power in me vested by the aforesaid act of Congress, do hereby proclaim and make known that on and alter July 2, 1924, and throughout the fiscal year 1924–1925, the quota of each nationality provided in said Act shall be as follows:

Country or area of birth	Quota 1924–1925		
Afghanistan	100	Egypt	100
Albania	100	Estonia	124
Andorra	100	Ethiopia (Abyssinia)	100
Arabian peninsula	100	Finland	170
Armenia	124	France	3,954
Australia, including Papua, Tasmania, and all islands appertaining to Australia	121	Germany	51,227
		Great Britain and Northern Ireland	34,007
Austria	785	Greece	100
Belgium	512	Hungary	473
Bhutan	100	Iceland	100
Bulgaria	100	India	100
Cameroon (proposed British mandate)	100	Iraq (Mesopotamia)	100
Cameroon (French mandate)	100	Irish Free State	28,567
China	100	Italy, including Rhodes, Dodekanesia, and Castellorizzo	3,845
Czechoslovakia	3,073	Japan	100
Danzig, Free City of	228	Latvia	142
Denmark	2,789	Liberia	100

Liechtenstein	100	Rumania	603
Lithuania	344	Russia, European and Asiatic	2,248
Luxemburg	100		
Monaco	100	Samoa, Western (proposed mandate of New Zealand)	100
Morocco (French and Spanish Zones and Tangier)	100	San Marino	100
		Siam	100
Muscat (Oman)	100	South Africa, Union of	100
Nauru (proposed British mandate)	100	South West Africa (proposed mandate of Union of South Africa)	100
Nepal	100		
Netherlands	1,648	Spain	131
New Zealand (including appertaining islands)	100	Sweden	9,561
		Switzerland	2,081
Norway	6,453	Syria and The Lebanon (French mandate)	100
New Guinea, and other Pacific Islands under proposed Australian mandate	100	Tanganyika (proposed British mandate)	100
Palestine (with Trans-Jordan, proposed British mandate)	100	Togoland (proposed British mandate)	100
Persia	100	Turkey	100
Poland	5,982	Yap and other Pacific islands (under Japanese mandate)	100
Portugal	1,503	Yugoslavia	671
Ruanda and Urundi (Belgium mandate)	100		

GENERAL NOTE—The immigration quotas assigned to the various countries and quota-areas should not be regarded as having any political significance whatever, or as involving recognition of new governments, or of new boundaries, or of transfers of territory except as the United States Government has already made such recognition in a formal and official manner. . . . ★

This photograph of an Italian immigrant family on Ellis Island was taken by Lewis Wickes Hine. His portraits of the immigrant life exposed the wretched housing and terrible working conditions that many immigrants were subjected to in their new homeland.

The 1924 restrictions

applied primarily to "new" immigrants from southern and eastern Europe, as well as to Asians and Africans. A congressional study made prior to the law's passing reported that these groups were "inferior, uneducated and posed a serious threat to American society." Restrictions on immigration did not apply to Mexico, Canada, or any other nation in North or South America.

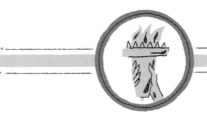

RESPONSE

The quota system immediately almost shut down immigration from eastern and southern Europe. Since most people who wanted to come to the United States were from those areas, the number of immigrants dropped dramatically. The Immigration Act of 1965 ended national quotas for immigration.

A photograph portrays immigrants arriving in New York Harbor from Hamburg, Germany, on the *SS Patricia* on December 10, 1906. This boat carried 162 first-class passengers, 184 second-class passengers, and 2,100 steerage passengers. The steerage section of a ship had the worst accommodations and was occupied by poorer passengers. Because the fare to the United States was so expensive, most immigrants traveled in steerage.

This 1917 poster from the Cleveland Board of Education and the Cleveland Americanization Committee used six languages—English, Italian, Slovene, Polish, Hungarian, and Yiddish—to advertise free classes where immigrants could "learn the language of America" and "prepare for American Citizenship." Before the 1880s, most immigrants had come from northern Europe. The similarity of their customs, language, and religion to those of earlier Americans made it fairly easy for them to fit into society. Later, more and more of the newcomers came from southern and eastern Europe, and their differences seemed greater to many Americans.

By the 1890s, Ellis Island, in New York City's harbor, became the major center for immigrants entering the United States.

Immigration again became a flashpoint issue early in the presidency of Donald Trump, when he issued executive orders temporarily banning immigrants from certain Muslim countries. In each instance, the bans were tried in court.

WAR MESSAGE TO CONGRESS

FRANKLIN DELANO ROOSEVELT

December 8, 1941

On Sunday, December 7, the Japanese launched a surprise air attack on the United States naval base at Pearl Harbor in Hawaii. More than 2,300 Americans died in the early-morning bombing, which also destroyed most of the Pacific air force fleet.

Americans were shocked, saddened, and outraged. The next day, President Roosevelt asked Congress to declare war on Japan. Later, the United States went to war with Japan's allies, Germany and Italy.

Many Americans had wanted the United States to enter the war from the time Nazi Germany invaded Poland in 1939. It became clear that Germany wanted to conquer Europe; Japan sought to control the Pacific area. Neither country was a democracy like the United States.

World War II ended in victory for the Allies. The United States and the Union of Soviet Socialist Republics (USSR) emerged as the world's two superpowers.

FDR'S WAR MESSAGE TO CONGRESS

Yesterday, December 7, 1941—a day which will live in infamy—the United States of America was suddenly and deliberately attacked by naval and air forces of the empire of Japan.

The United States was at peace with that nation and, at the solicitation of Japan, was still in conversation with its government and its emperor looking toward the maintenance of peace in the Pacific.

Indeed, one hour after Japanese air squadrons had commenced bombing in the American Island of Oahu the Japanese Ambassador to the United States and his colleague delivered to our Secretary of State a formal reply to a recent American message. And. while this reply stated that it seemed useless to continue the existing diplomatic negotiations, it contained no threat or hint of war or of armed attack.

It will be recorded that the distance of Hawaii from Japan makes it obvious that the attack was deliberately planned many days or even weeks ago. During the intervening time the Japanese Government has deliberately sought to deceive the United States by false statements and expressions of hope for continued peace.

The attack yesterday on the Hawaiian Islands has caused severe damage to American naval and military forces. I regret to tell you that very many American lives have been lost. In addition American ships have been reported torpedoed on the high seas between San Francisco and Honolulu.

Yesterday the Japanese Government also launched an attack against Malaya.

Last night Japanese forces attacked Hong Kong.

Last night Japanese forces attacked Guam.

Last night Japanese forces attacked the Philippine Islands.

Last night the Japanese attacked Wake Island.

And this morning the Japanese attacked Midway Island.

Japan has therefore undertaken a surprise offensive extending throughout the Pacific area. The facts of yesterday and today speak for themselves. The people of the United States have already formed their opinions and well understand the implications to the very life and safety of our nation.

As Commander in Chief of the Army and the Navy, I have directed that all measures be taken for our defense.

Always will our whole nation remember the character of the onslaught against us.

No matter how long it may take us to overcome this premeditated invasion, the American people in their righteous might will win through to absolute victory.

I believe that I interpret the will of the Congress and of the people when I assert that we will not only defend ourselves to the uttermost but will make it very certain that this form of treachery shall never again endanger us. Hostilities exist. There is no blinking at the fact that our people, our territory and our interests are in grave danger. With confidence in our armed forces, with the unbounding determination of our people, we will gain the inevitable triumph. So help us God.

I ask that Congress declare that since the unprovoked and dastardly attack by Japan on Sunday, December 7, 1941, a state of war has existed between the United States and the Japanese Empire. ★

A dramatic photo shows the *USS California* sinking after the surprise attack at Pearl Harbor on December 7, 1941. Months later, the sunken ship was refloated and repaired. The *California* went on to win seven battle stars in World War II.

A worker in California reads the news of Pearl Harbor. The attack shocked Americans. Sixteen-year-old Mary Ann Ramsey, the daughter of Navy Commander Logan C. Ramsey, watched the injured come in and recalled, "With the first sailor, so horribly burned, personal fear left me; he brought me the full tragedy of the day."

Out of the war came a new technology of destruction—the atom bomb, which the United States secretly developed and then dropped on the Japanese cities of Hiroshima and Nagasaki in 1945 to force Japan to surrender.

By the morning of December 8, the White House was on the alert in case of a surprise attack. Before the president read his war message, the White House staff was being fitted for gas masks, blackout curtains were being measured to cover the windows, and extra police had surrounded the building.

A day before the attack on Pearl Harbor, the president learned that the Japanese had rejected any attempt to resolve differences between America and Japan. Roosevelt then said, "This means war."

AUTHOR

After the United States entered World War II, Franklin Roosevelt proved to be a skilled commander in chief. As it became increasingly clear that the Allies would defeat Germany and Japan, he prepared the nation to assume the leadership of the postwar world. Exhausted by his efforts overseeing the war, Roosevelt died in April 1945. The only president to be elected four times, he was mourned by the entire nation.

RESPONSE

At 12:30 in the afternoon of December 8, Franklin Delano Roosevelt read his war message to Congress. The nation immediately united under the president's leadership. Congress voted almost unanimously to declare war against Japan. Three days later, Germany and Italy declared war against the United States. America had entered World War II.

President Roosevelt signed the declaration of war against Japan just one day after the surprise attack on Pearl Harbor.

President Roosevelt wrote his war message almost entirely by himself. Fueled by his outrage about the attack on Pearl Harbor, he wrote swiftly. He had been advised to write a long description of Japanese behavior that led him to this point. Instead, the president decided on a brief message.

Before the attack on Pearl Harbor, an American code expert had cracked the Japanese diplomatic code. American military experts now knew that the Japanese were up to something. But they expected them to target Southeast Asia, perhaps in the Philippines.

The most famous words in Roosevelt's war message were not in his original draft. That draft read, "Yesterday, December 7, 1941, a date which will live in world history. . ." Almost immediately, he scratched out this wording and substituted, "a date which will live in infamy."

BROWN v. BOARD of EDUCATION

May 17, 1954

In 1954, it was the law in 17 southern and border states that African-American and white children attend separate public schools. Four other states segregated students by school districts. All these states justified their policy by saying that black and white schools were "separate but equal," meaning that they were racially separated, but equal in accommodations and in educational opportunity. This phrase was the essence of an 1896 Supreme Court decision, *Plessy v. Ferguson*, in which the right of states to pass laws allowing racial segregation was held to be constitutional.

In 1954 the National Association for the Advancement of Colored People (NAACP) challenged the "separate but equal" doctrine at the elementary school level. NAACP lawyers argued before the Supreme Court that children in all-white schools received a better education than children in all-black schools. In May 1954 the Court agreed and outlawed racial segregation in public schools. Because of the Brown decision, African-American and white children, as well as children of all other races and ethnicities, today can legally attend the same public schools.

The Brown case was joined with four other suits from other parts of the country, shown here in this memorandum brief. But because the Brown case was listed first, their joint case was called *Brown v. Board of Education of Topeka*.

BROWN V. BOARD OF EDUCATION OF TOPEKA

These cases come to us from the states of Kansas, South Carolina, Virginia, and Delaware. They are premised on different facts and different local conditions, but a common legal question justifies their consideration together in this consolidated opinion.

In each of the cases, minors of the Negro race, through their legal representatives, seek the aid of the courts in obtaining admission to the public schools of their community on a non-segregated basis. In each instance, they have been denied admission to schools attended by white children under laws requiring or permitting segregation according to race. This segregation was alleged to deprive the plaintiffs of the equal protection of the laws under the Fourteenth Amendment. In each of the cases other than the Delaware case, a three-judge federal district court denied relief to the plaintiffs on the so-called "separate but equal" doctrine announced by this Court in *Plessy v. Ferguson* [famous 1896 decision that declared social segregation of whites and blacks was legal]. . . . Under that doctrine, equality of treatment is accorded when the races are provided substantially equal facilities, even though these facilities be separate. . . .

The plaintiffs contend that segregated public schools are not "equal" and cannot be made "equal," and that hence they are deprived of the equal protection of the laws. Because of the obvious importance of the question presented, the Court took jurisdiction. . . .

There are findings below that the Negro and white schools involved have been equalized, or are being equalized, with respect to buildings, curricula, qualifications, and salaries of teachers, and other "tangible" factors. Our decision, therefore, cannot turn on merely a comparison of these tangible factors in the Negro and white schools involved in each of the cases. We must look instead to the effect of segregation itself on public education.

In approaching this problem, we cannot turn the clock back to 1868 when the Amendment was adopted, or even to 1896 when *Plessy v. Ferguson* was written. We must consider public education in the light of its full development and its present place in American life throughout the nation. Only in this way can it be determined if segregation in public schools deprives these plaintiffs of the equal protection of the laws.

Today, education is perhaps the most important function of state and local governments. Compulsory school attendance laws and the great expenditures for education both demonstrate our recognition of the importance of education to our democratic society. It is required in the performance of our most basic public responsibilities, even service in the armed forces. It is the very foundation of good citizenship. Today it is a principal instrument in awakening the child to cultural values, in preparing him for later professional training, and in helping him to adjust normally to his environment. In these days, it is doubtful that any child may reasonably be expected to succeed in life if he is denied the opportunity of an education. Such an opportunity, where the state has undertaken to provide it, is a right which must be made available to all on equal terms.

We come then to the question presented: Does segregation of children in public schools solely on the basis of race, even though the physical facilities and other "tangible" factors may be equal, deprive the children of the minority group of equal educational opportunities? We believe that it does. . . .

To separate them from others of similar age and qualifications solely because of their race generates a feeling of inferiority as to their status in the community that may affect their hearts and minds in a way unlikely ever to be undone. The effect of this separation on their educational opportunities was well stated by a finding in the Kansas case by a court which nevertheless felt compelled to rule against the Negro plaintiffs:

"Segregation of white and colored children in public schools has a detrimental effect upon the colored children. The impact is greater when it has the sanction of the law; for the policy of separating the races is usually interpreted as denoting the inferiority of the Negro group. A sense of inferiority affects the motivation of a child to learn. Segregation with the sanction of law, therefore, has a tendency to retard the educational and mental development of Negro children and to deprive them of some of the benefits they would receive in a racially integrated school system."

Whatever may have been the extent of psychological knowledge at the time of *Plessy v. Ferguson,* this finding is amply supported by modern authority. Any language in *Plessy v. Ferguson* contrary to this finding is rejected.

We conclude that in the field of public education the doctrine of "separate but equal" has no place. Separate educational facilities are inherently unequal. Therefore, we hold that the plaintiffs and others similarly situated for whom the actions have been brought are, by reason of the segregation complained of, deprived of the equal protection of the laws guaranteed by the Fourteenth Amendment. . . . ★

Thurgood Marshall was one of the NAACP lawyers who argued the Brown case before the Supreme Court. Called "Mr. Civil Rights" for his heroic efforts to end segregation, Marshall argued 32 cases before the Supreme Court, winning 29. In 1967 he became the first African-American appointed to the Supreme Court.

In 1957 President Dwight Eisenhower called out federal troops to protect African-American students attempting to attend previously all-white Central High School in Little Rock, Arkansas. Angry white students are shown here harassing and shouting insults at Elizabeth Eckford.

The Brown in the case was Oliver Brown. He lived in Topeka, Kansas, which had segregated schools. Brown was angry that his eight-year-old daughter had to travel by bus to a black school even though the family lived only three blocks from an all-white public school.

In the Brown case, the Court held that education had become a key part of what it meant to be a citizen. Success in the work force and in life depended on it. Therefore, the Court ruled, if a state is to provide universal education, it must be made available equally to both blacks and whites. Separate, segregated schools failed to do this, the Court held.

Six African-American teens who had attended Little Rock's Central High School in 1957–1958 sit with NAACP chief counsel Thurgood Marshall and Arkansas NAACP president Daisy Lee Gatson Bates outside the Supreme Court in this August 22, 1958, photo. From left to right are Melba Patillo, 16; Jefferson Thomas, 15; Gloria Ray, 15; Mrs. Bates; Thurgood Marshall; Carlotta Walls, 15; Minnijean Brown, 16; and Elizabeth Eckford, 16.

The attorneys for the plaintiffs in the *Brown* case used many arguments to support their belief that segregated schools were unfair and unlawful. The most important of these was that segregated schools were a violation of the "equal protection" clause of the Fourteenth Amendment (see p. 94). The justices agreed with the plaintiffs, and *Plessy v. Ferguson* was overturned. Many people regard this case as the beginning of the Civil Rights movement.

Justice Earl Warren felt that the decision would have a more powerful effect if all the judges agreed. But two judges held out. Warren used all his political skills on them, and the final decision was unanimous.

AUTHOR

Earl Warren (1891–1974) was the fourteenth chief justice of the Supreme Court. A three-term governor of California, Warren was appointed chief justice by President Dwight D. Eisenhower in 1953. Warren proved to be a forceful leader. The Warren Court's decisions moved the nation closer to racial and social equality. This made him controversial. Many Americans applauded him, and Justice William O. Douglas called him "one of our three greatest Chief Justices." But some critics said he was too liberal and tried unsuccessfully to remove him from his position. In 1969 Earl Warren retired from the Court.

RESPONSE

Although some school districts did integrate their schools quickly, most Southern states refused to obey the ruling. So the next year the Supreme Court ordered the states to move forward "with all deliberate speed" to school black and white students together. Federal judges had to push reluctant Southern school districts and some northern schools to desegregate. In the cases where resistance was severe, the National Guard was called in to insure the safety of students in newly desegregated schools (see photo, p. 139).

Earl Warren grew up in Bakersfield, California, and graduated from the University of California at Berkeley. He served in World War I and was a county district attorney before becoming governor of California in 1942.

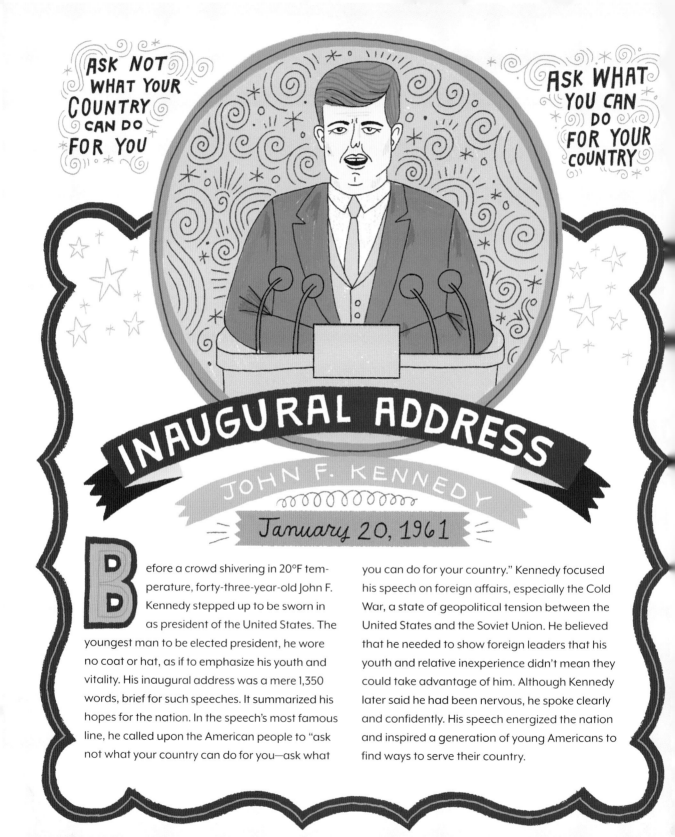

ASK NOT WHAT YOUR COUNTRY CAN DO FOR YOU

ASK WHAT YOU CAN DO FOR YOUR COUNTRY

INAUGURAL ADDRESS

JOHN F. KENNEDY

January 20, 1961

Before a crowd shivering in 20°F temperature, forty-three-year-old John F. Kennedy stepped up to be sworn in as president of the United States. The youngest man to be elected president, he wore no coat or hat, as if to emphasize his youth and vitality. His inaugural address was a mere 1,350 words, brief for such speeches. It summarized his hopes for the nation. In the speech's most famous line, he called upon the American people to "ask not what your country can do for you—ask what you can do for your country." Kennedy focused his speech on foreign affairs, especially the Cold War, a state of geopolitical tension between the United States and the Soviet Union. He believed that he needed to show foreign leaders that his youth and relative inexperience didn't mean they could take advantage of him. Although Kennedy later said he had been nervous, he spoke clearly and confidently. His speech energized the nation and inspired a generation of young Americans to find ways to serve their country.

INAUGURAL ADDRESS

We observe today not a victory of party but a celebration of freedom—symbolizing an end as well as a beginning—signifying renewal as well as change. For I have sworn before you and Almighty God the same solemn oath our forebears prescribed nearly a century and three-quarters ago.

The world is very different now. For man holds in his mortal hands the power to abolish all forms of human poverty and all forms of human life. And yet the same revolutionary beliefs for which our forebears fought are still at issue around the globe—the belief that the rights of man come not from the generosity of the state but from the hand of God.

We dare not forget today that we are the heirs of that first revolution. Let the word go forth from this time and place, to friend and foe alike, that the torch has been passed to a new generation of Americans—born in this century, tempered by war, disciplined by a hard and bitter peace, proud of our ancient heritage—and unwilling to witness or permit the slow undoing of those human rights to which this nation has always been committed, and to which we are committed today at home and around the world.

Let every nation know, whether it wishes us well or ill, that we shall pay any price, bear any burden, meet any hardship, support any friend, oppose any foe to assure the survival and the success of liberty.

This much we pledge—and more.

To those old allies whose cultural and spiritual origins we share, we pledge the loyalty of faithful friends. United, there is little we cannot do in a host of cooperative ventures. Divided, there is little we can do—for we dare not meet a powerful challenge at odds and split asunder.

To those new states whom we welcome to the ranks of the free, we pledge our word that one form of colonial control shall not have passed away merely to be replaced by a far more iron tyranny. We shall not always expect to find them supporting our view. But we shall always hope to find them strongly supporting their own freedom—and to remember that, in the past, those who foolishly sought power by riding the back of the tiger ended up inside.

To those people in the huts and villages of half the globe struggling to break the bonds of mass misery, we pledge our best efforts to help them help themselves, for whatever period is required—not because the Communists may be doing it, not because we seek their votes, but because it is right. If a free society cannot help the many who are poor, it cannot save the few who are rich.

To our sister republics south of the border, we offer a special pledge—to convert our good words into good deeds—in a new alliance for progress—to assist free men and free governments in casting off the chains of poverty. But this peaceful revolution of hope cannot become the prey of hostile powers. Let all our neighbors know that we shall join with them to oppose aggression or subversion anywhere in the Americas. And let every other power know that this hemisphere intends to remain the master of its own house.

To that world assembly of sovereign states, the United Nations, our last best hope in an age where the instruments of war have far outpaced the instruments of peace, we renew our pledge of support—to prevent it from becoming merely a forum for invective—to strengthen its shield of the new and the weak—and to enlarge the area in which its writ may run.

Finally, to those nations who would make themselves our adversary, we offer not a pledge but a request: that both sides begin anew the quest for peace, before the dark powers of destruction unleashed by science engulf all humanity in planned or accidental self-destruction.

We dare not tempt them with weakness. For only when our arms are sufficient beyond doubt can we be certain beyond doubt that they will never be employed.

But neither can two great and powerful groups of nations take comfort from our present course— both sides overburdened by the cost of modern weapons, both rightly alarmed by the steady spread of the deadly atom, yet both racing to alter that uncertain balance of terror that stays the hand of mankind's final war.

So let us begin anew—remembering on both sides that civility is not a sign of weakness, and sincerity is always subject to proof. Let us never negotiate out of fear. But let us never fear to negotiate.

Let both sides explore what problems unite us instead of belaboring those problems which divide us.

Let both sides, for the first time, formulate serious and precise proposals for the inspection and control of arms—and bring the absolute power to destroy other nations under the absolute control of all nations.

Let both sides seek to invoke the wonders of science instead of its terrors. Together let us explore the stars, conquer the deserts, eradicate disease, tap the ocean depths, and encourage the arts and commerce.

Let both sides unite to heed in all corners of the earth the command of Isaiah—to "undo the heavy burdens . . . [and] let the oppressed go free."

And if a beachhead of cooperation may push back the jungle of suspicion, let both sides join in creating a new endeavor, not a new balance of power, but a new world of law, where the strong are just and the weak secure and the peace preserved.

All this will not be finished in the first one hundred days. Nor will it be finished in the first one thousand days, nor in the life of this administration, nor even perhaps in our lifetime on this planet. But let us begin.

In your hands, my fellow citizens, more than mine, will rest the final success or failure of our course. Since this country was founded, each generation of Americans has been summoned to give testimony to its national loyalty. The graves of young Americans who answered the call to service surround the globe.

Now the trumpet summons us again—not as a call to bear arms, though arms we need—not as a call to battle, though embattled we are—but a call to bear the burden of a long twilight struggle, year in and year out, "rejoicing in hope, patient in tribulation"—a struggle against the common enemies of man: tyranny, poverty, disease, and war itself.

Can we forge against these enemies a grand and global alliance, North and South, East and West, that can assure a more fruitful life for all mankind? Will you join in that historic effort?

In the long history of the world, only a few generations have been granted the role of defending freedom in its hour of maximum danger. I do not shrink from this responsibility—I welcome it. I do not believe that any of us would exchange places with any other people or any other generation. The energy, the faith, the devotion which we bring to this endeavor will light our country and all who serve it—and the glow from that fire can truly light the world.

And so, my fellow Americans: ask not what your country can do for you—ask what you can do for your country.

My fellow citizens of the world: ask not what America will do for you, but what together we can do for the freedom of man.

Finally, whether you are citizens of America or citizens of the world, ask of us here the same high standards of strength and sacrifice which we ask of you. With a good conscience our only sure reward, with history the final judge of our deeds, let us go forth to lead the land we love, asking His blessing and His help, but knowing that here on earth God's work must truly be our own. ★

John Fitzgerald Kennedy took the oath of office as the thirty-fifth president of the United States on January 20, 1961. Although Kennedy was the youngest man elected president, he was not the youngest in American history. Theodore Roosevelt was 279 days younger than Kennedy when he became president after the assassination of William McKinley.

President Kennedy plays in the Oval Office in 1962 with his two children. John Jr. and Caroline. Kennedy's administration brought a breath of youth and glamour to the presidency. John Jr. and Caroline were the youngest children of a president to live in the White House in more than 60 years.

The president-elect decided to make his address short. Explained Kennedy, "I don't want people to think I'm a windbag."

Kennedy asked Theodore Sorenson, his speechwriter, to discover "the secret" of Lincoln's Gettysburg Address (see p. 90), which he hoped to use as a model. The speechwriter reported to him, "Lincoln never used a two- or three-syllable word where a one-syllable word would do, and never used two or three words where one word would do."

AUTHOR

John F. Kennedy (1917–1963) was the thirty-fifth president. Born into a wealthy Massachusetts Irish-American family, he was the first Catholic ever elected president. In the closest election since 1884, the Democratic senator from Massachusetts squeaked past Republican Vice President Richard Nixon by only 100,000 votes. During the campaign Kennedy promised voters a "New Frontier." His New Frontier included such programs as more federal aid to education and increased funding to NASA, the space agency.

Once in office, Kennedy had a hard time getting Congress to support his goals. Many New Frontier programs were not passed because of the opposition of conservative Southern Democrats in Congress who thought his goals were too liberal. Yet some New Frontier programs were enacted. One of the most popular, the Peace Corps, sent thousands of volunteers—mostly young people—to help in underdeveloped countries. Kennedy's term was cut short when he was assassinated in Dallas by Lee Harvey Oswald on November 22, 1963.

RESPONSE

Americans were captivated by the image of the young, handsome, dynamic president. Around the world, his speech won praise for its idealistic and inspiring tone. Young people especially responded to Kennedy's assertion that "a torch has been passed" to a younger generation, and to his promises to fight poverty and injustice. Many were inspired to join the Peace Corps or otherwise enter public service. Allies of the United States were relieved that Kennedy promised steadfast support "to assure the survival and success of liberty" while also toning down the hostile words of the Cold War and offering a fresh start at the negotiating table to the Soviets. Many civil rights leaders were disappointed that Kennedy hadn't focused on the injustices faced by black Americans.

President Dwight D. Eisenhower (right) with his successor, John F. Kennedy (left) walk together at the presidential retreat at Camp David, Maryland.

The morning of his inauguration Kennedy arose early and, in between bites of breakfast, practiced the speech aloud to make it sound just right.

No Kennedy speech, Theodore Sorensen, Kennedy's chief speechwriter later recalled, "ever underwent so many drafts." Sorensen destroyed his original draft of the speech at the request of Jacqueline Kennedy, but he insisted throughout his life that Kennedy was the principal author of all his speeches, including the inaugural.

THE DECLARATION of INDIAN PURPOSE

June 20, 1961

In June 1961 Native American activists met at a nationwide Indian Conference in Chicago. The delegates drafted a Declaration of Indian Purpose to protest the government's termination policy. This policy, begun in 1953, allowed Congress to "terminate" a tribe by making a law saying that the tribe no longer legally or politically existed. Between 1954 and 1962 Congress terminated more than 60 tribes, most of them in the West. The delegates believed that the termination policy was a way for the government to claim Indian lands for itself or for corporate interests. The declaration asked Congress to change course completely. Rather than disbanding tribes, the federal government was asked to help Native Americans preserve and develop their own communities.

The Declaration was an early part of a widespread Native American movement to defend Indian rights and retain tribal lands and ways of life. In a series of decisions, the Supreme Court returned a large part of tribal independence, lands, and artifacts. This process continues today. The following passage is from the declaration.

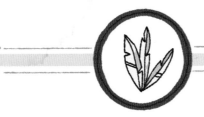

THE DECLARATION OF INDIAN PURPOSE

STATEMENT OF PURPOSE:

. . . In order to give recognition to certain basic philosophies by which the Indian People live, We, the Indian People, must be governed by principles in a democratic manner with a right to choose our way of life. Since our Indian culture is threatened by presumption of being absorbed by the American society, we believe we have the responsibility of preserving our precious heritage. We believe that the Indians must provide the adjustment and thus freely advance with dignity to a better life. . . .

CREED:

We believe in the inherent right of all people to retain spiritual and cultural values, and that the free exercise of these values is necessary to the normal development of any people. Indians exercised this inherent right to live their own lives for thousands of years before the white man came and took their lands. It is a more complex world in which Indians live today, but the Indian people who first settled the New World and built the great civilizations which only now are being dug out of the past, long ago demonstrated that they could master complexity.

We believe that the history and development of America show that the Indian has been subjected to duress, undue influence, unwarranted pressures, and policies which have produced uncertainty, frustration, and despair. Only when the public understands these conditions and is moved to take action toward the formulation and adoption of sound and consistent policies and programs will these destroying factors be removed and the Indian resume his normal growth and make his maximum contribution to modern society.

We believe in the future of a greater America, an America which we were first to love, where life, liberty, and the pursuit of happiness will be a reality. In such a future, with Indians and all other Americans cooperating, a cultural climate will be created in which the Indian people will grow and develop as members of a free society.

CONCLUDING STATEMENT:

To complete our Declaration, we point out that in the beginning the people of the New World, called Indians by accident of geography, were possessed of a continent and a way of life. In the course of many lifetimes, our people had adjusted to every climate and condition from the Arctic to the torrid zones. In their livelihood and family relationships, their ceremonial observances, they reflected the diversity of the physical world they occupied.

The conditions in which Indians live today reflect a world in which every basic aspect of life has been transformed. Even the physical world is no longer the controlling factor in determining where and under what conditions men may live. In region after region, Indian groups found their means of existence either totally destroyed or materially modified. Newly introduced diseases swept away or reduced regional populations. These changes were followed by major shifts in the internal life of tribe and family.

The time came when the Indian people were no longer the masters of their situation. Their life ways survived subject to the will of a dominant sovereign power. This is said, not in a spirit of complaint; we understand that in the lives of all nations of people, there are times of plenty and times of famine. But we do speak out in a plea for understanding.

When we go before the American people, as we do in this Declaration, and ask for material assistance in developing our resources and developing our opportunities, we pose a moral problem which cannot be left unanswered. For the problem we raise affects the standing which our nation sustains before world opinion.

Our situation cannot be relieved by appropriated funds alone, though it is equally obvious that without capital investment and funded services, solutions will be delayed. Nor will the passage of time lessen the complexities which beset a people moving toward new meaning and purpose.

The answers we seek are not commodities to be purchased, neither are they evolved automatically through the passing of time.

The effort to place social adjustment on a money-time interval scale which has characterized Indian administration, has resulted in unwanted pressure and frustration.

When Indians speak of the continent they yielded, they are not referring only to the loss of some millions of acres in real estate. They have in mind that the land supported a universe of things they knew, valued, and loved.

With that continent gone, except for the few poor parcels they still retain, the basis of life is precariously held, but they mean to hold the scraps and parcels as earnestly as any small nation or ethnic group was ever determined to hold to identity and survival.

What we ask of America is not charity, not paternalism, even when benevolent. We ask only that the nature of our situation be recognized and made the basis of policy and action.

In short, the Indians ask for assistance, technical and financial, for the time needed, however long that may be, to regain in the America of the space age some measure of the adjustment they enjoyed as the original possessors of their native land. ★

AUTHORS

About 700 Native Americans from 64 tribes took part in the congress. They drafted, debated, and passed the Declaration of Indian Purpose with the goal of having a greater voice in shaping their destiny.

RESPONSE

The delegates made themselves heard. By the early 1960s, the government ended its termination policy. Many young Indians were inspired to become organizers and were able to win additional gains for Native Americans in the coming decades.

In 2011, Native American activists urged President Obama not to allow construction of the Keystone XL Pipeline through tribal lands. President Obama listened to them and rejected the pipeline. President Trump reversed Obama's decision in 2017.

In 1973 Native American militants took control of the village at Wounded Knee, South Dakota. This photograph shows them surrounding a car carrying the Assistant Attorney General from a meeting with militant leaders.

Non-Indians could attend some meetings of the conference, but only as silent observers.

The government made one-time payments to terminated tribes in exchange for their lands. These payments were divided among the members of the former tribes. For the most part, these payments were small and many Indians had to take low-paying jobs or depend on government services to survive.

One Indian wept as his tribe signed a contract giving the tribe's best land in North Dakota to the government. He said, "The members of the tribal council sign this contract with heavy hearts."

SILENT SPRING

RACHEL CARSON
1962

Since World War II, author and scientist Rachel Carson had studied and written about the interconnectedness of all living things and the strength of natural systems like the ocean. She became worried about powerful insecticides such as DDT and their effects on humans, wildlife, and the earth's environment after learning of large numbers of animals dying in areas where DDT had been used.

DDT was developed during World War II primarily to eliminate malaria-carrying mosquitoes in the South Pacific. Later, agricultural businesses used it and other pesticides extensively on crops without taking into account the harm they were doing to other animals, including humans. In *Silent Spring,* Carson eloquently voiced her concerns. *Silent Spring* was one of the most influential books in the second half of the twentieth century. It launched the environmental movement in the United States. Carson's book also alerted people worldwide to the dangers of industrial environmental pollution. The following passage is from *Silent Spring.*

SILENT SPRING

. . . It took hundreds of millions of years to produce the life that now inhabits the earth—eons of time in which that developing and evolving and diversifying life reached a state of adjustment and balance with its surroundings. The environment, rigorously shaping and directing the life it supported, contained elements that were hostile as well as supporting. Certain rocks gave out dangerous radiation; even within the light of the sun, from which all life draws its energy, there were short-wave radiations with power to injure. Given time—time not in years, but in millennia—life adjusts, and a balance has been reached. For time is the essential ingredient; but in the modern world there is no time.

The rapidity of change and the speed with which new situations are created follow the impetuous and heedless pace of man rather than the deliberate pace of nature. Radiation is no longer merely the background radiation of rocks, the bombardment of cosmic rays, the ultraviolet of the sun that have existed before there was any life on earth; radiation is now the unnatural creation of man's tampering with the atom. The chemicals to which life is asked to make its adjustment are no longer merely the calcium and silica and copper and all the rest of the minerals washed out of the rocks and carried in rivers to the sea; they are the synthetic creations of man's inventive mind, brewed in his laboratories, and having no counterparts in nature.

To adjust to these chemicals would require time on the scale that is nature's; it would require not merely the years of a man's life but the life of generations. And even this, were it by some miracle possible, would be futile, for the new chemicals come from our laboratories in an endless stream; almost five hundred annually find their way into actual use in the United States alone. The figure is staggering and its implications are not easily grasped—500 new chemicals to which the bodies of men and animals are required somehow to adapt each year, chemicals totally outside the limits of biologic experience.

Among them are many that are used in man's war against nature. Since the mid-1940s over 200 basic chemicals have been created for use in killing insects, weeds, rodents, and other organisms described in the modern vernacular as "pests" and they are sold under several thousand different brand names.

➤

These sprays, dusts, and aerosols are now applied almost universally to farms, gardens, forests, and homes—nonselective chemicals that have the power to kill every insect, the "good" and the "bad," to still the song of birds and the leaping of fish in the streams, to coat the leaves with a deadly film, and to linger on in the soil—all this though the intended target may be only a few weeds or insects. Can anyone believe it is possible to lay down such a barrage of poisons on the surface of the earth without making it unfit for all life? They should not be called "insecticides," but "biocides."

The whole process of spraying seems caught up in an endless spiral. Since DDT was released for civilian use, a process of escalation has been going on in which ever more toxic materials must be found. This has happened because insects, in a triumphant vindication of Darwin's principle of the survival of the fittest, have evolved super races immune to the particular insecticide used, hence a deadlier one has always to be developed—and then a deadlier one than that. . . .

The "control of nature" is a phrase conceived in arrogance, born of the Neanderthal age of biology and philosophy, when it was supposed that nature exists for the convenience of man. The concepts and practices of applied entomology for the most part date from that Stone Age of science. It is our alarming misfortune that so primitive a science has armed itself with the most modern and terrible weapons, and that in turning them against the insects it has also turned them against the earth. ★

Crop-dusting planes sprayed pesticides over acres of land. Because of the harmful effects of poisonous pesticides such as DDT, new insecticides have been developed that control pests while causing less damage to the environment.

In 1951 Carson published

The Sea Around Us, which described the history, chemistry, biology, and ecology of the sea. This book, which was translated into many languages, made her famous. In all her writings, she emphasized the interrelation of living things and how the welfare of humans depends on the welfare of all the natural world. An editor said about Rachel Carson, "A few thousand words from her and the world took a new direction."

AUTHOR

Rachel Carson (1907–1964) was a biologist and writer. Born in Pennsylvania, her childhood interest in wildlife led Carson to attend Johns Hopkins University. She taught zoology at the University at Maryland until 1936. Carson then went to work for many years as a marine biologist for the United States Fish and Wildlife Service. Carson knew that her book would be controversial, and that the powerful chemical and agricultural industries would attack her. Her background as a scientist and her meticulous research allowed her to bravely face down her opponents.

RESPONSE

Silent Spring became a bestseller. The agricultural and chemical industries, however, were infuriated by what they saw as an attack against their practices. They struck back, blasting the book and throwing their support behind those who disagreed with Carson. President Kennedy ordered the President's Science Advisory Committee to study the questions raised in the book about DDT and the overuse of pesticides. The committee reported that *Silent Spring* and its author were right. As a result, DDT came under much closer government supervision.

Today, *Silent Spring* is recognized as one of the founding documents of the environmental movement. It helped lead to the formation of the Environmental Protection Agency (EPA) in 1970 and to a ban on DDT in 1972.

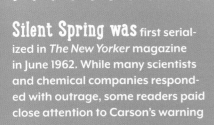

Silent Spring was first serialized in *The New Yorker* magazine in June 1962. While many scientists and chemical companies responded with outrage, some readers paid close attention to Carson's warning about the dangers of chemical pesticides. Congressman John Lindsay inserted portions of the *New Yorker* article into the Congressional Record.

Carson once wrote, "The beauty of the living world I was trying to save has always been uppermost in my mind. . . . Now I can believe I have at least helped a little."

"ICH BIN EIN BERLINER"

SPEECH AT BERLIN WALL

JOHN F. KENNEDY

June 26, 1963

After World War II, the German city of Berlin was divided. The Soviets controlled East Berlin, while England, France, and the United States controlled West Berlin. In August 1961 the Russians suddenly closed the border between East and West Berlin. They also built a concrete-and-barbed-wire wall to stop East Germans from fleeing to the West. But people kept on trying anyway; some even died in the attempt. Two years later, President John F. Kennedy made a speech at the wall. His point was simple: if anyone had any doubts as whether the Soviet system was working, come to Berlin and look at this wall. To show his solidarity with the people of Berlin, he proclaimed, "Ich bin ein Berliner" ("I am a Berliner").

Kennedy's speech by the Berlin Wall is considered one of his best. Little did he or his listeners know that 26 years later, the Communist East German government would open the wall and allow its citizens to leave freely—see p. 188.

SPEECH AT THE BERLIN WALL

Two thousand years ago the proudest boast was "Civitas Romanus sum." ["I am a Roman citizen."] Today, in the world of freedom, the proudest boast is "Ich bin ein Berliner."

There are many people in the world who really don't understand, or say they don't, what is the great issue between the free world and the Communist world. Let them come to Berlin. There are some who say that Communism is the wave of the future. Let them come to Berlin. And there are some who say in Europe and elsewhere we can work with the Communists. Let them come to Berlin. And there are even a few who say that it is true that Communism is an evil system, but it permits us to make economic progress. "Lasst sie nach Berlin kommen." ["Let them come to Berlin."]

Freedom has many difficulties and democracy is not perfect, but we have never had to put a wall up to keep our people in, to prevent them from leaving us. I want to say, on behalf of my countrymen, who live many miles away on the other side of the Atlantic, who are far distant from you, that they take the greatest pride that they have been able to share with you, even from a distance, the story of the last eighteen years. I know of no town, no city, that has been besieged for eighteen years that still lives with the vitality and the force, and the hope and the determination of the city of West Berlin. While the wall is the most obvious and vivid demonstration of the failures of the Communist system, for all the world to see, we take no satisfaction in it, for it is an offense not only against history but an offense against humanity, separating families, dividing husbands and wives and brothers and sisters, and dividing a people who wish to be joined together.

What is true of this city is true of Germany—real, lasting peace in Europe can never be assured as long as one German out of four is denied the elementary right of free men, and that is to make a free choice. In eighteen years of peace and good faith, this generation of Germans has earned the right to be free, including the right to unite their families and their nation in lasting peace with good will to all people. You live in a defended island of freedom, but your life is part of the main. So let me ask you, as I close, to lift your eyes beyond the dangers of today to the hopes of tomorrow, beyond the freedom merely of this city of Berlin, or your country of Germany, to the advance of freedom everywhere, beyond the wall to the day of peace with justice, beyond yourselves and ourselves to all mankind. Freedom is indivisible, and when one man is enslaved, all are not free. When all are free, then we can look forward to that day when this city will be joined as one—and this country, and this great continent of Europe—in a peaceful and hopeful glow. When that day finally comes, as it will, the people of West Berlin can take sober satisfaction in the fact that they were in the front lines for almost two decades.

All free men, wherever they may live, are citizens of Berlin, and therefore, as a free man, I take pride in the words "Ich bin ein Berliner." ★

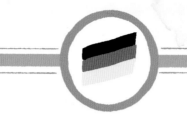

President John F. Kennedy addresses a crowd of more than 300,000 West Berliners at Schoneberg Town, proudly proclaiming "Ich bin ein Berliner." Although one possible German translation means "I am a jelly doughnut" in local slang, Kennedy did in fact say, "I am a Berliner," and the crowd cheered his efforts.

West Berlin was bordered by East Berlin on one side, and on the other three sides by East German territory. It was essentially a landlocked island. The border between East and West Berlin was the easiest way for East Germans to escape to the West—until the wall was constructed.

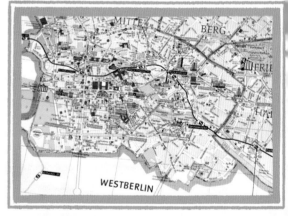

The Soviets erected the Berlin Wall in 1961 to stop the large exodus of people fleeing East Berlin for the non-Communist world. Between 1949 and July 1961 at least 2.7 million people fled East Germany, many of them through West Berlin.

Around the time Kennedy spoke at the Berlin Wall, the Americans and Soviets set up a telephone hotline so that leaders of each country could speak directly to each other during any crises, hoping to avert unnecessary hostilities.

Shortly after President Kennedy's death in November of 1963, the square where he had made his "Ich bin ein Berliner" speech was renamed the John F. Kennedy Platz.

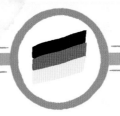

AUTHOR

Throughout his short presidency, John F. Kennedy dealt with Cold War tensions between the United States and the Soviet Union. In April 1961 he supported an unsuccessful attempt by exiled Cubans to overthrow the Communist government in Cuba. The next year, worried that the Soviets were stockpiling missiles in Cuba (during what came to be known as the Cuban Missile Crisis), he demanded that they be removed. The Soviets backed down and shipped the missiles back to Russia. During Kennedy's term, he also sent more American advisers to Asia, particularly to Vietnam, to help save the anti-Communist government of South Vietnam, which was engaged in a civil war with Vietnamese

Communists known as the Viet Cong. On November 22, 1963, Kennedy was assassinated in Dallas, Texas. Vice President Lyndon B. Johnson succeeded him. Johnson's Great Society program put into effect many of the social reforms that had been proposed by John F. Kennedy.

RESPONSE

The Western powers hailed President Kennedy's speech, as did the American people and the media. Kennedy had succeeded in shifting the Cold War confrontation from military threats to a focus on freedom and self-determination for a captive people. Two months after his Berlin speech, the United States, Great Britain, and the Soviet Union signed the Limited Nuclear Test Ban Treaty.

This photograph shows Kennedy touring Checkpoint Charlie, the main crossing point from East to West Berlin and back, maintained by United States forces.

Two months before he spoke at the Berlin Wall, President Kennedy began to think about ways of easing the Cold War. He said that both sides had been "caught up in a vicious cycle in which suspicion on one side breeds suspicion on the other."

"I HAVE a DREAM..."

THE MARCH ON WASHINGTON ADDRESS

MARTIN LUTHER KING, JR.

August 28, 1963

As summer 1963 drew to a close, a crowd of about 250,000 Americans from all walks of life gathered at the Lincoln Memorial to rally for jobs and racial justice. At the end of a day of stirring songs and speeches, Martin Luther King, Jr., rose to speak. Although he gave many eloquent speeches during his life, the March on Washington Address was one of King's most memorable. In an era when Jim Crow laws were commonly in effect, relegating blacks to second-class citizenship, King's speech summed up the hopes and dreams of the young but growing civil rights movement. Using peaceful means—the power of the word, of marches, of boycotts, and when necessary, of nonviolent civil disobedience—King and his fellow civil rights leaders sought to end segregation and racial discrimination, and bring true equality to black Americans. Most Americans today instantly recognize the speech's most famous line, "I have a dream."

MARCH ON WASHINGTON ADDRESS

Five score years ago, a great American, in whose symbolic shadow we stand, signed the Emancipation Proclamation. This momentous decree came as a great beacon light of hope to millions of Negro slaves who had been seared in the flames of withering injustice. It came as a joyous daybreak to end the long night of captivity.

But one hundred years later, we must face the tragic fact that the Negro is still not free. One hundred years later, the life of the Negro is still sadly crippled by the manacles of segregation and the chains of discrimination. One hundred years later, the Negro lives on a lonely island of poverty in the midst of a vast ocean of material prosperity. One hundred years later, the Negro is still languishing in the corners of American society and finds himself an exile in his own land. So we have come here today to dramatize an appalling condition.

In a sense we have come to our nation's Capital to cash a check. When the architects of our republic wrote the magnificent words of the Constitution and the Declaration of Independence, they were signing a promissory note to which every American fell heir. This note was a promise that all men would be guaranteed the unalienable rights of life, liberty, and the pursuit of happiness.

It is obvious today that America has defaulted on this promissory note insofar as her citizens of color are concerned. Instead of honoring this sacred obligation, America has given the Negro people a bad check; a check which has come back marked "insufficient funds." But we refuse to believe that the bank of justice is bankrupt. We refuse to believe that there are insufficient funds in the great vaults of opportunity of this nation. So we have come to cash this check—a check that will give us upon demand the riches of freedom and the security of justice.

We have also come to this hallowed spot to remind America of the fierce urgency of now. This is not time to engage in the luxury of cooling off or to take the tranquilizing drug of gradualism. Now is the time to make real the promises of democracy. Now is the time to rise from the dark and desolate valley of segregation to the sunlit path of racial justice. Now is the time to open the doors of opportunity to all of God's children. Now is the time to lift our nation from the quicksands of racial injustice to the solid rock of brotherhood.

It would be fatal for the nation to overlook the urgency of the moment and to underestimate the determination of the Negro. This sweltering summer of the Negro's legitimate discontent will not pass until there is an invigorating autumn of freedom and equality. Nineteen sixty-three is not an end, but a beginning. Those who hope that the Negro needed to blow off steam and will now be content will have a rude awakening if the nation returns to business as usual. There will be neither rest nor tranquillity in America until the Negro is granted his citizenship rights. The whirlwinds of revolt will continue to shake the foundations of our nation until the bright day of justice emerges.

But there is something that I must say to my people who stand on the warm threshold which leads into the palace of justice. In the process of gaining our rightful place we must not be guilty of wrongful deeds. Let us not seek to satisfy our thirst for freedom by drinking from the cup of bitterness and hatred. We must forever conduct our struggle on the high plane of dignity and discipline. We must not allow our creative protest to degenerate into physical violence. Again and again we must rise to the majestic heights of meeting physical force with soul force.

The marvelous new militancy which has engulfed the Negro community must not lead us to a distrust of all white people, for many of our white brothers, as evidenced by their presence here today, have come to realize that their freedom is inextricably bound to our freedom. We cannot walk alone.

And as we walk, we must make the pledge that we shall march ahead. We cannot turn back. There are those who are asking the devotees of civil rights, "When will you be satisfied?"

We can never be satisfied as long as the Negro is the victim of the unspeakable horrors of police brutality.

We can never be satisfied as long as our bodies, heavy with fatigue of travel, cannot gain lodging in the motels of the highways and the cities.

We cannot be satisfied as long as the Negro's basic mobility is from a smaller ghetto to a larger one.

We can never be satisfied as long as a Negro in Mississippi cannot vote and a Negro in New York believes he has nothing for which to vote.

No, no, we are not satisfied, and we will not be satisfied until justice rolls down like waters and righteousness like a mighty stream.

I am not unmindful that some of you have come here out of great trials and tribulations. Some of you have come fresh from narrow jail cells. Some of you have come from areas where your quest for freedom left you battered by the storms of persecution and staggered by the winds of police brutality. You have been the veterans of creative suffering. Continue to work with the faith that unearned suffering is redemptive.

Go back to Mississippi, go back to Alabama, go back to South Carolina, go back to Georgia, go back to Louisiana, go back to the slums and ghettos of our Northern cities, knowing that somehow this situation can and will be changed. Let us not wallow in the valley of despair.

I say to you today, my friends, that in spite of the difficulties and frustrations of the moment I still have a dream. It is a dream deeply rooted in the American dream.

I have a dream that one day this nation will rise up and live out the true meaning of its creed: "We hold these truths to be self-evident; that all men are created equal."

I have a dream that one day on the red hills of Georgia the sons of former slaves and the sons of former slaveowners will be able to sit down together at the table of brotherhood.

I have a dream that one day even the state of Mississippi, a desert state sweltering with the heat of injustice and oppression, will be transformed into an oasis of freedom and justice.

I have a dream that my four little children will one day live in a nation where they will not be judged by the color of their skin but by the content of their character.

I have a dream today.

I have a dream that one day the state of Alabama, whose governor's lips are presently dripping with the words of interposition and nullification, will be transformed into a situation where little black boys and black girls will be able to join hands with little white boys and girls and walk together as sisters and brothers.

I have a dream today.

I have a dream that one day every valley shall be exalted, every hill and mountain shall be made low, the rough places will be made plain, and the crooked places will be made straight, and the glory of the Lord shall be revealed, and all flesh shall see it together.

This is our hope. This is the faith with which I return to the South. With this faith we will be able to hew out of the mountain of despair a stone of hope. With this faith we will be able to transform the jangling discords of our nation into a beautiful symphony of brotherhood.

With this faith we will be able to work together, to pray together, to struggle together, to go to jail together, to stand up for freedom together, knowing that we will be free one day.

This will be the day when all of God's children will be able to sing with new meaning, "My country 'tis of thee, sweet land of liberty, of thee I sing. Land where my father died, land of the Pilgrims' pride, from every mountainside, let freedom ring."

And if America is to be a great nation, this must become true. So let freedom ring from the prodigious hilltops of New Hampshire. Let freedom ring from the mighty mountains of New York. Let freedom ring from the heightening Alleghenies of Pennsylvania!

Let freedom ring from the snowcapped Rockies of Colorado! Let freedom ring from the curvaceous peaks of California! But not only that; let freedom ring from Stone Mountain of Georgia! Let freedom ring from Lookout Mountain of Tennessee!

Let freedom ring from every hill and molehill of Mississippi. From every mountainside, let freedom ring.

When we let freedom ring, when we let it ring from every village and every hamlet, from every state and every city, we will be able to speed up that day when all of God's children, black men and white men, Jews and Gentiles, Protestants and Catholics, will be able to join hands and sing in the words of the old Negro spiritual, "Free at last! Free at last! Thank God Almighty, we are free at last!" ★

Civil rights leaders met with President Kennedy on the day of the 1963 March on Washington. From left to right: Mathew Ahmann (National Catholic Conference for Interracial Justice); Whitney Young (National Urban League); Martin Luther King, Jr.(SCLC); John Lewis (SNCC); Rabbi Joachim Prinz (American Jewish Congress); Reverend Eugene Carson Blake (United Presbyterian Church); A. Philip Randolph; President John F. Kennedy; Walter Reuther (labor leader), with Vice President Lyndon Johnson partially visible behind him; and Roy Wilkins (NAACP).

The African-American spiritual "We Shall Overcome" was the anthem of the civil rights movement.

As he was speaking to the thousands who had gathered to hear him at the Lincoln Memorial in Washington, D.C., Martin Luther King, Jr., extemporized—invented on the spot—the most famous part of his speech in response to a shout from gospel singer Mahalia Jackson: "Tell them about the dream, Martin!"

AUTHOR

Born in Atlanta, Martin Luther King, Jr., (January 15, 1929–April 4, 1968) established his leadership in the civil rights movement as pastor of the Dexter Avenue Baptist Church in Montgomery, Alabama. Among many other actions, he was an organizer of the Montgomery bus boycott, which ended when the U.S. Supreme Court ruled that laws requiring segregation on city buses were unconstitutional. In the years following the "I Have a Dream" speech, King remained committed to nonviolence, despite mounting criticism inside the civil rights movement. He was awarded the Nobel Peace Prize in 1964, at 35 the youngest man to have been so honored. In early 1968 he began a "Poor People's Campaign" to deal with economic problems, and he spoke out against American involvement in the Vietnam War. On April 4, 1968, while in Memphis, Tennessee, to support striking sanitation workers, King was assassinated. His birthday, January 15, has become a national holiday.

With an estimated crowd of 250,000, the March on Washington was, according to King, "the greatest demonstration of freedom in the history of our nation."

RESPONSE

The "I Have a Dream" speech was seen by live television audiences throughout the United States. In October 1963 Congress began deliberating on the Civil Rights Act. The bill, which passed in 1964, ended legal segregation in public places such as lunch counters and hotels and outlawed discrimination in employment by race, color, sex, religion, or national origin. It also guaranteed equal protection of the right to vote, and gave the government the power to sue to desegregate public places such as museums and schools.

On April 3, King made a speech in Memphis in which he seemed to foresee his own death. King said, "We've got some difficult days ahead, but it really doesn't matter to me now, because I've been to the mountaintop." The next evening a sniper killed him while he stood on his motel balcony.

The idea for the March on Washington originated with A. Philip Randolph, a founder of the Brotherhood of Sleeping Car Porters and the Negro American Labor Council.

THE BALLOT OR THE BULLET

MALCOLM X

April 3, 1964

Some civil rights activists grew impatient with the nonviolent tactics of civil disobedience favored by Martin Luther King, Jr., and other leaders of the movement. They urged African-Americans to take control of their own communities and to rely on direct action and self-defense. Malcolm X was the most forceful voice of what became known as the Black Power movement. In early April, he spoke before the Congress of Racial Equality (CORE), an important civil rights organization. Malcolm X warned there would be another kind of march on Washington if Congress delayed passing civil rights legislation. This angry and compelling speech with its message of black pride has helped make Malcolm X a hero to many Americans.

THE BALLOT OR THE BULLET

So, what I'm trying to impress upon you, in essence, is this: You and I in America are faced not with a segregationist conspiracy, we're faced with a government conspiracy. . . . You don't have anybody putting blocks in your path but people who are a part of the government. The same government that you go abroad to fight for and die for is the government that is in a conspiracy to deprive you of your voting rights, deprive you of your economic opportunities, deprive you of decent housing, deprive you of decent education. You don't need to go to the employer alone, it is the government itself, the government of America, that is responsible for the oppression and exploitation and degradation of black people in this country. And you should drop it in their lap. This government has failed the Negro. This so-called democracy has failed the Negro. And all these white liberals have definitely failed the Negro.

So where do we go from here? First, we need some friends. We need some new allies. The entire civil-rights struggle needs a new interpretation, a broader interpretation. We need to look at this civil-rights thing from another angle—from the inside as well as from the outside. To those of us whose philosophy is black nationalism, the only way you can get involved in the civil-rights struggle is give it a new interpretation. That old interpretation excluded us. It kept us out. So, we're giving a new interpretation to the civil-rights struggle, an interpretation that will enable us to come into it, take part in it. And these handkerchief-heads who have been dillydallying and pussyfooting and compromising— we don't intend to let them pussyfoot and dillydally and compromise any longer.

How can you thank a man for giving you what's already yours? How then can you thank him for giving you only part of what's already yours? You haven't even made progress, if what's being given to you, you should have had already. That's not progress. And I love my Brother Lomax [Louis Lomax, a leader of the civil rights group, the Congress of Racial Equality (CORE)], the way he pointed out we're right back where we were in 1954. We're behind where we were in 1954. We're not even as far up as we were in 1954. There's more segregation now than there was in 1954. There's more racial animosity, more racial hatred, more racial violence today in 1964, than there was in 1954. Where is the progress?

And now you're facing a situation where the young Negro's coming up. They don't want to hear that "turn-the-other-cheek" stuff, no. In Jacksonville, those were teenagers, they were throwing Molotov cocktails. Negroes have never done that before. But it shows you there's a new deal coming in. There's new thinking coming in. There's new strategy coming in. It'll be Molotov cocktails this month, hand grenades next month, and something else next month. It'll be ballots, or it'll be bullets. It'll be liberty, or it will be death. The only difference about this kind of death—it'll be reciprocal. You know what is meant by "reciprocal"? That's one of Brother Lomax's words, I stole it from him. I don't usually deal with those big words because I don't usually deal with big people. I deal with small people. I find you can get a whole lot of small people and whip hell out of a whole lot of big people. They haven't got anything to lose, and they've got everything to gain. And they'll let you know in a minute: "It takes two to tango; when I go, you go."

The black nationalists, those whose philosophy is black nationalism, in bringing about this new interpretation of the entire meaning of civil rights, look upon it as meaning, as Brother Lomax has pointed out, equality of opportunity. Well, we're justified in seeking civil rights, if it means equality of opportunity, because all we're doing there is trying to collect for our investment. Our mothers and fathers invested sweat and blood. Three hundred and ten years we worked in this country without a dime in return—I mean without a dime in return. You let the white man walk around here talking about how rich this country is, but you never stop to think how it got rich so quick. It got rich because you made it rich.

You take the people who are in this audience right now. They're poor, we're all poor as individuals. Our weekly salary individually amounts to hardly anything. But if you take the salary of everyone in here collectively it'll fill up a whole lot of baskets. It's a lot of wealth. If you can collect the wages of just these people right here for a year, you'll be rich—richer than rich. When you look at it like that, think how rich Uncle Sam had to become, not with this handful, but millions of black people. Your and my mother and father, who didn't work an eight-hour shift, but worked from "can't see" in the morning until "can't see" at night, and worked for nothing, making the white man rich, making Uncle Sam rich.

This is our investment. This is our contribution—our blood. Not only did we give of our free labor, we gave of our blood. Every time he had a call to arms, we were the first ones in uniform. We died on every battlefield the white man had. We have made a greater sacrifice than anybody who's standing up in America today. We have made a greater contribution and have collected less. Civil rights, for those of us whose philosophy is black nationalism, means "Give it to us now. Don't wait for next year. Give it to us yesterday, and that's not fast enough. . . ."

If you don't take this kind of stand, your little children will grow up and look at you and think "shame." If you don't take an uncompromising stand—I don't mean go out and get violent; but at the same time you should never be nonviolent unless you run into some nonviolence. I'm nonviolent with those who are nonviolent with me. But when you drop that violence on me, then you've made me go insane, and I'm not responsible for what I do. And that's the way every Negro should get. Any time you know you're within the law, within your legal rights, within your moral rights, in accord with justice, then die for what you believe in. But don't die alone. Let your dying be reciprocal. This is what is meant by equality. What's good for the goose is good for the gander. . . .

If a Negro in 1964 has to sit around and wait for some cracker [poor southern white] senator to filibuster when it comes to the rights of black people, why, you and I should hang our heads in shame. You talk about a march on Washington in 1963, you haven't seen anything. There's some more going down in '64. And this time they're not going like they went last year. They're not going singing "We Shall Overcome." They're not going with white friends. They're not going with placards already painted for them. They're not going with round-trip tickets. They're going with one-way tickets.

And if they don't want that nonviolent army going down there, tell them to bring the filibuster to a halt. The black nationalists aren't going to wait. Lyndon B. Johnson is the head of the Democratic Party. If he's for civil rights, let him go into the Senate next week and declare himself. Let him go in there right now and declare himself. Let him go in there and denounce the Southern branch of his party. Let him go in there right now and take a moral stand—right now, not later. Tell him, don't wait until election time. If he waits too long, brothers and sisters, he will be responsible for letting a condition develop in this country which will create a climate that will bring seeds up out of the ground with vegetation on the end of them looking like something these people never dreamed of. In 1964, it's the ballot or the bullet. Thank you.

Malcolm X is shown here in May 1963 addressing a Harlem rally in support of integration efforts in Birmingham, Alabama. Malcolm X wrote, "The black race here in North America is in extremely bad condition. You show me a black man who isn't an extremist, and I'll show you one who needs psychiatric attention."

Many young African-Americans were impatient with the nonviolent tactics of Martin Luther King, Jr. These young people made up what came to be called the Black Power movement. This photograph shows teenagers and children lifting their fists in the Black Power salute outside their school in San Francisco in 1969.

Malcolm X visited Cairo, Egypt, in July 1964 for the African Summit Conference. Here, he points out passages in the Koran to another attendee.

After a 1964 pilgrimage to Mecca, the holy city of the Islamic religion, Malcolm X left behind his black separatist views and focused on accomplishing social change through community action.

In 1964, after Malcolm X left the Nation of Islam and made a holy pilgrimage to Mecca, he took the Arabic name El-Hajj Malik El-Shabazz—though he is still known to the world as Malcolm

X. When he returned from Mecca, Malcolm said he had met "blonde-haired, blued-eyed men I could call my brothers," and had begun to consider racial integration a viable hope for the future.

AUTHOR

Malcom X (1925–1965), the son of a Baptist preacher, was born Malcolm Little in Omaha, Nebraska. At the age of twenty-one he was sentenced to six years in jail for burglary. While in prison, Malcolm converted to the Nation of Islam, a religion that advocates complete separation from white society. (Members of the Nation of Islam have also been called Black Muslims.) Articulate and charismatic, Malcolm became the national spokesman for the Nation of Islam. His growing mistrust of Elijah Muhammad, the Nation of Islam's leader, led to a rift that caused Malcolm to break with the sect. He was assassinated by Black Muslims on February 25, 1965, during a speech in Harlem.

RESPONSE

For many African-Americans, especially young people in the northern cities, the speech reinforced their self-respect. Frustrated by what they saw as the slow pace of change brought about through the nonviolent tactics of leaders like Martin Luther King, Jr., they were attracted to the more militant position of Malcolm X. In contrast, many whites were frightened and angered by what they saw as Malcolm X's threat of violence by African-Americans. In the summer of 1965 such violence did erupt when African-Americans rioted in Los Angeles, and again in 1967 in Newark, New Jersey, and Detroit, Michigan.

In April 1964, Malcolm X made a pilgrimage to Mecca in April 1964. There he met with Prince Faisal al-Saud, who later became the king of Saudi Arabia.

Malcolm X was a popular speaker on college campuses. Both white and African-American students flocked to hear his condemnation of "Whitism," or white supremacy.

The X in Malcolm X stood for the stolen identity of African slaves.

Less than a year after this speech, Malcolm X was murdered. At his funeral, actor Ossie Davis gave the eulogy and called him "our own black shining prince."

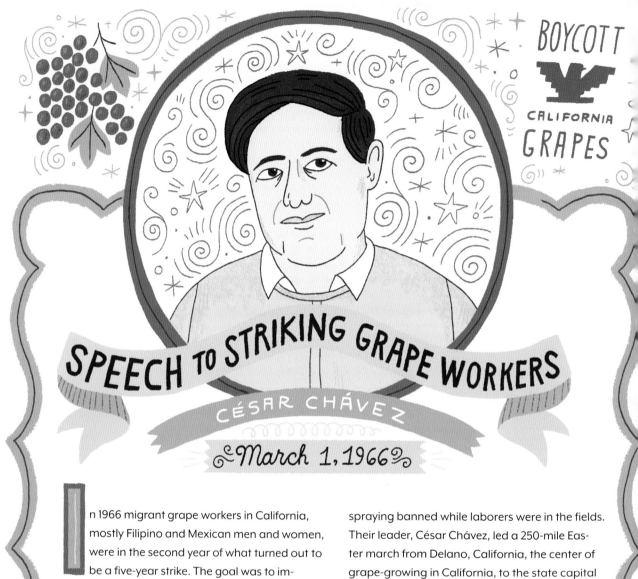

BOYCOTT

CALIFORNIA
GRAPES

SPEECH TO STRIKING GRAPE WORKERS

CÉSAR CHÁVEZ

March 1, 1966

In 1966 migrant grape workers in California, mostly Filipino and Mexican men and women, were in the second year of what turned out to be a five-year strike. The goal was to improve the poor working conditions and wages of migrant farm laborers. The grape workers made an average of $0.90 per hour. Their average life expectancy in 1966 was forty-nine years. Child labor was common and many laborers were injured or died due to poor working and living conditions. The striking workers demanded rest periods, clean drinking water and hand-washing facilities, and, because they came into contact with chemical pesticides while working, they wanted pesticide spraying banned while laborers were in the fields. Their leader, César Chávez, led a 250-mile Easter march from Delano, California, the center of grape-growing in California, to the state capital at Sacramento. When the marchers reached the capital, Chávez delivered this short speech. By the end of the 1960s his efforts had helped farm workers, and especially Mexican-Americans, to organize politically. In 1969, the United Farm Workers had enough clout to lead a nationwide boycott of grapes, pressuring growers to accept the union. Chávez's leadership helped call attention to discrimination against Mexican-Americans and win support for laws to require equal treatment.

SPEECH TO STRIKING GRAPE WORKERS

"In the 'March from Delano to Sacramento' there is a meeting of cultures and traditions; the centuries-old religious tradition of Spanish culture conjoins with the very contemporary cultural syndrome of "demonstration" springing from the spontaneity of the poor, the downtrodden, the rejected, the discriminated against bearing visibly their need and demand for equality and freedom.

In every religion-oriented culture "the pilgrimage" has had a place: a trip made with sacrifice and hardship as an expression of penance and of commitment—and often involving a petition to the patron of the pilgrimage for some sincerely sought benefit of body or soul. Pilgrimage has not passed from Mexican culture. Daily at any of the major shrines of the country and in particular at the Basilica of the Lady of Guadalupe, there arrive pilgrims from all points—some of whom may have long since walked out the pieces of rubber tire that once served them as soles, and many of whom will walk on their knees the last mile or so of the pilgrimage. Many of the "pilgrims" of Delano will have walked such pilgrimages themselves in their lives—perhaps as very small children even—and cling to the memory of the day-long marches, the camps at night, streams forded, hills climbed, the sacral aura of the sanctuary, and the "fiesta" that followed.

But throughout the Spanish-speaking world there is another tradition that touches the present march, that of the Lenten penitential processions, where the penitentes would march through the streets, often in sack cloth and ashes, some even carrying crosses, as a sign of penance for their sins, and as a plea for the mercy of God. The penitential procession is also in the blood of the Mexican American, and the Delano march will therefore be one of penance—public penance for the sins of the strikers, their own personal sins as well as their yielding perhaps to feelings of hatred and revenge in the strike itself. They hope by the march to set themselves at peace with the Lord, so that the justice of their cause will be purified of all lesser motivation.

These two great traditions of a great people meet in the Mexican American with the belief that Delano is his "cause," his great demand for justice, freedom, and respect from a predominantly foreign cultural community in a land where he was first. The revolutions of Mexico were primarily uprisings of the poor, fighting for bread and for dignity. The Mexican-American is also a child of the revolution.

Pilgrimage, penance and revolution. The pilgrimage from Delano to Sacramento has strong religio-cultural overtones. But it is also the pilgrimage of a cultural minority which has suffered from a hostile environment, and a minority which means business.

César Chávez leads a march demanding that California grape growers recognize the United Farm Workers Union and promoting an economic boycott of table grapes grown in California. The Gallo Winery was one of the leading growers' biggest customers.

In another speech César Chávez asked, "How long will it be before we take seriously the importance of the workers who harvest the food we eat?"

A migrant worker is a person who moves from place to place to get work. Many farm workers are migrants, following the harvests for different crops in different locations.

Influenced by Chávez, other Mexican-American leaders began to work for bilingual educational programs to improve language skills and economic and social opportunities for their people.

This speech is commonly called "God Is Beside you on the Picket Line."

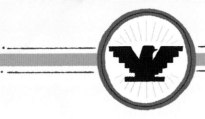

AUTHOR

César Chávez (1927–1993) was the founder and leader of the United Farm Workers of America. He was born in Arizona to immigrant parents who lost their family farm during the Depression and were forced to become migrant workers. In 1962 Chávez decided to devote all his energies to organizing a union for farmworkers. Chávez used the same tactics as the civil rights movement, such as nonviolence, boycotts, sit-ins, and marches. When in 1968 frustrated union members threatened to resort to violence, Chávez went on a public fast that lasted 25 days, ending the threat.

The union he founded, the first union of migratory workers in the United States, is still active today.

RESPONSE

César Chávez began winning nationwide attention for his cause. In 1969 Americans of all ethnicities sup- ported the strikers by joining in a nationwide boycott of California grapes. A year later, the largest of the grape growers finally recognized the union. In 1975, the landmark Agricultural Labor Relations Act was passed in California, guaranteeing farm workers the right to organize, vote in state-supervised secret- ballot elections, and bargain with their employers.

This poster advertises a 1968 performance in support of the United Farm Workers Union to be held at New York City's Carnegie Hall. Fund- raisers like this increased both financial resources and visibility for the union. The largest growers agreed to recognize the union in 1969.

When Senator Robert F. Kennedy participated in hearings of the Senate Subcommittee on Migratory Labor in March 1966, he heard the Kern County (which includes Delano) Sheriff relate how his deputies arrested peaceful picketers because they were being threatened by struck growers. Kennedy suggested to the sheriff and and the district attorney that they read the Constitution of the United States!

During their struggle to unionize, 95 percent of the strikers lost their homes and their cars because they had no work.

THE EAGLE HAS LANDED

～July 21, 1969～

In 1961 President John F. Kennedy promised to beat the Soviets in the space race by landing an astronaut on the moon before the decade's end. Eight years later, the lunar module of Apollo 11 gently touched down near the moon's Sea of Tranquility. Astronaut Neil Armstrong stepped onto the moon's surface, becoming the first human being to walk on the moon.

The moon landing was one of the highlights of American space exploration, which continues to the present. The excitement of seeing humans walk on the moon has never been matched, and it helped establish America's scientific, technological, and economic leadership in the world.

At the time, space exploration was considered by many to be a front in the Cold War: if the United States didn't get there first, the Soviets would. Competition between the United States and the Soviet Union—to be the first to successfully launch a satellite, to put an astronaut in orbit, the first to send a manned spacecraft to another planet—was fierce. After the Soviets had successfully put the Sputnik satellite in orbit, Americans were fearful of losing the "space race." People on both sides of the Iron Curtain feared the militarization of space.

This excerpt is from a three-way conversation among Armstrong, his fellow astronaut Edwin "Buzz" Aldrin, Jr., and flight control center in Houston, Texas, (identified here as Duke) during the landing.

THE EAGLE HAS LANDED

102:45:43 Armstrong (onboard): Shutdown.

102:45:44 Aldrin: Okay. Engine Stop.

102:45:45 Aldrin: ACA out of Detent.

102:45:46 Armstrong: Out of Detent. Auto. [The control stick was moved away from its centered position.]

102:45:47 Aldrin: Mode Control, both Auto. Descent Engine Command Override, Off. Engine Arm, Off. 413 is in. [413 is computer data that tells that the lunar module has landed.]

102:45:57 Duke: We copy you down, Eagle.

102:45:58 Armstrong (onboard): Engine arm is off. (Pause) Houston, Tranquility Base here. The Eagle has landed.

102:46:06 Duke: Roger, Tranquility. We copy you on the ground. You got a bunch of guys about to turn blue. We're breathing again. Thanks a lot.

102:46:16 Aldrin: Thank you.

102:46:18 Duke: You're looking good here. ★

This picture, taken from the lunar module, shows the astronauts planting the United States flag on the surface of the moon. Neil Armstrong stands on the left, and astronaut Buzz Aldrin stands on the right.

About 600 million people around the world watched the moon landing and walk on television. The American flag placed on the moon's surface has this message on it: "We come in peace for all mankind."

In 1961 the Soviet Union sent the first man into space. Americans believed that they needed to catch up to and surpass the Soviets. With more money put into the United States space agency (NASA), American astronauts went on a series of space missions, called the Mercury and Gemini projects, to explore space. What NASA learned from these earlier missions paved the way for the Apollo program and the moon landing.

ASTRONAUTS

Neil Armstrong (1930–2012) was born in Ohio. In 1949 he became a navy pilot. Armstrong joined the astronaut program in 1962 and retired in 1971. He received the Presidential Medal of Freedom in 1969. Edwin "Buzz" Aldrin, Jr., (b. 1930) was born in New Jersey. During the Korean War he flew combat missions. He was selected as an astronaut in 1963 and retired in 1971. Aldrin received the Exceptional Service Medal for his achievements as an astronaut.

RESPONSE

People around the world were riveted by the moon landing. It made headlines in newspapers across the planet, and congratulations poured in to the White House and to NASA from nearly every nation (the Soviet Union and China were exceptions). The triumph gave Americans, pummeled by the recent assassinations of Robert Kennedy and Martin Luther King, Jr., and news of the ongoing Vietnam War, something to celebrate and to renew optimism. Critics of the space program thought that the enormous amount of money spent on it should have gone into other programs.

Apollo 11 astronauts Neil Armstrong, Michael Collins, and Buzz Aldrin pose in their spacesuits for the official crew photo.

The focus of space exploration has changed since the Apollo days. Now the National Aeronautics and Space Administration (NASA) focuses primarily on sending unmanned probes into space such as the Voyager missions to Mars, Cassini to Saturn, Curiosity to Mars, and the Hubble Space Telescope. An international consortium of nations including the United States, Russia, Japan, Canada, and the European Space Agency conducts experiments aboard the International Space Station.

As he stepped on the moon, Neil Armstrong said, "That's one small step for man, one giant leap for mankind."

I'D RATHER BE BLACK THAN FEMALE

SHIRLEY CHISHOLM

1970

In 1968 Shirley Chisholm became the first African-American woman elected to the U.S. House of Representatives.

Two years later, in her autobiography, *Unbought and Unbossed,* she described the obstacles she had to overcome to succeed in the political world. She concluded that prejudice against women held her back more than racism. Many feminists felt that Shirley Chisholm was right and that if women wanted to gain more power in American society, they needed to get elected to political office. In the following years, more and more women ran for political office. Sixteen years after Chisholm's election, Geraldine Ferraro became the first woman to be the vice-presidential candidate of a major political party. In 1992, the first African-American woman, Carol Moseley Braun, was elected to the U.S. Senate. Hillary Clinton became the first female major party candidate for president in 2016.

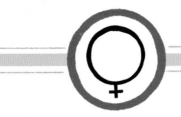

I'D RATHER BE BLACK THAN FEMALE

Being first black woman elected to Congress has made me some kind of phenomenon. There are nine other blacks in Congress; there are ten other women. I was the first to overcome both handicaps at once. Of the two handicaps, being black is much less of a drawback than being female.

If I said that being black is a greater handicap than being a woman, probably no one would question me. Why? Because "we all know" there is prejudice against black people in America. That there is prejudice against women is an idea that still strikes nearly all men—and, I am afraid, most women—as bizarre.

Prejudice against blacks was invisible to most white Americans for many years. When blacks finally started to "mention" it, with sit-ins, boycotts, and freedom rides, Americans were incredulous. "Who, us?" they asked in injured tones. "We're prejudiced?" It was the start of a long, painful reeducation for white America. It will take years for whites—including those who think of themselves as liberals—to discover and eliminate the racist attitude they all actually have.

How much harder will it be to eliminate the prejudice against women? I am sure it will be a longer struggle. Part of the problem is that women in America are much more brain-washed and content with their roles as second-class citizens than blacks ever were.

Let me explain. I have been active in politics for more than twenty years. For all but the last six, I have done the work—all the tedious details that make the difference between victory and defeat on election day—while men reaped the rewards, which is almost invariably the lot of women in politics.

It is still women—about three million volunteers—who do most of this work in the American political world. The best any of them can hope for is the honor of being district or county vice chairman, a kind of separate-but-equal position with which a woman is rewarded for years of faithful envelope stuffing and card-party organizing. In such a job, she gets a number of free trips to state and sometimes national meetings and conventions, where her role is supposed to be to vote the way her male chairman votes.

When I tried to break out of that role in 1963 and run for the New York State Assembly seat from Brooklyn's Bedford-Stuyvesant, the resistance was bitter. From the start of that campaign, I faced undisguised hostility because of my sex.

But it was four years later, when I ran for Congress, that the question of my sex became a major issue. Among members of my own party, closed meetings were held to discuss ways of stopping me. . . .

When a bright young woman graduate starts looking for a job, why is the first question always: "Can you type?" A history of prejudice lies behind that question. Why are women thought of as secretaries, not administrators? Librarians and teachers, but not doctors and lawyers? Because they are thought of as different and inferior. The happy homemaker and the contented darky are both stereotypes produced by prejudice.

Women have not even reached the level of tokenism that blacks are reaching. No women sit on the Supreme Court. Only two have held Cabinet rank and none do at present. Only two women hold ambassadorial rank. But women predominate in the lower-paying, menial, unrewarding, dead-end jobs, and when they do reach better positions, they are invariably paid less than a man gets for the same job.

If that is not prejudice, what would you call it?

A few years ago, I was talking with a political leader about a promising young woman as a candidate. "Why invest time and effort to build the girl up?" he asked me. "You know she'll only drop out of the game to have a couple of kids just about the time we're ready to run her for mayor."

Plenty of people have said similar things about me. Plenty of others have advised me, every time I tried to take another upward step, that I should go back to teaching, a woman's vocation, and leave politics to the men. I love teaching, and I am ready to go back to it as soon as I am convinced that this country no longer needs a woman's contribution.

When there are no children going to bed hungry in this rich nation, I may be ready to go back to teaching. When there is a good school for ever child, I may be ready. When we do not spend our wealth on hardware to murder people, when we no longer tolerate prejudice against minorities, and when the laws against unfair housing and unfair employment practices are enforced "instead of evaded, then there may be nothing more for me to do in politics.

But until that happens—and we all know it will not be this year or next—what we need is more women in politics, because we have a very special contribution to make. I hope that the example of my success will convince other women to get into politics—and not just to stuff envelopes, but to run for office.

It is women who can bring empathy, tolerance, insight, patience, and persistence to government—the qualities we naturally have or have had to develop because of our suppression by men. The women of a nation mold its morals, its religion, and its politics by the lives they live. At present, our country needs women's idealism and determination, perhaps more in politics than anywhere else. ★

AUTHOR

Shirley Chisholm (1924–2005) was born in Brooklyn, New York. First a teacher, then a politician, she represented her Brooklyn district in Congress for seven terms, retiring in 1982. While in Congress, she was an outspoken critic of the Vietnam War, and a strong advocate for federal economic support for cities, education, and of civil rights. In 1972 she became the first African-American to campaign for the Democratic party nomination for president. On the first nominating ballot, she received more than 150 delegate votes, far higher than expectations. When asked how she wanted to be remembered, Chisholm said, "I don't want to be remembered as the first black woman who went to Congress. And I don't even want to be remembered as the first woman who happened to be black to make the bid for the presidency. I want to be remembered as a woman who fought for change in the 20th century. That's what I want."

RESPONSE

Chisholm's outspokenness served her well as a trailblazer and as an agent for change, but it hampered her as a legislator. Many of her male colleagues, perhaps envious of the high profile she had gained during her presidential bid, refused to cooperate with her. Her leadership and her writing, however, inspired younger women to run for office and speak out against discrimination.

Congresswoman Shirley Chisholm shakes hands with civil rights pioneer Rosa Parks at an event.

Chisholm cofounded the National Women's Political Caucus in 1971, and in 1984 helped start the National Political Congress for Black Women. The new organization's goal was to encourage African-American women to run for political office.

Shirley Chisholm said about her campaign to be the Democratic presidential nominee, "I began to open the way for women to think they can run."

Chisholm announced her backing of Senator George McGovern after she lost her bid to be the Democratic presidential candidate.

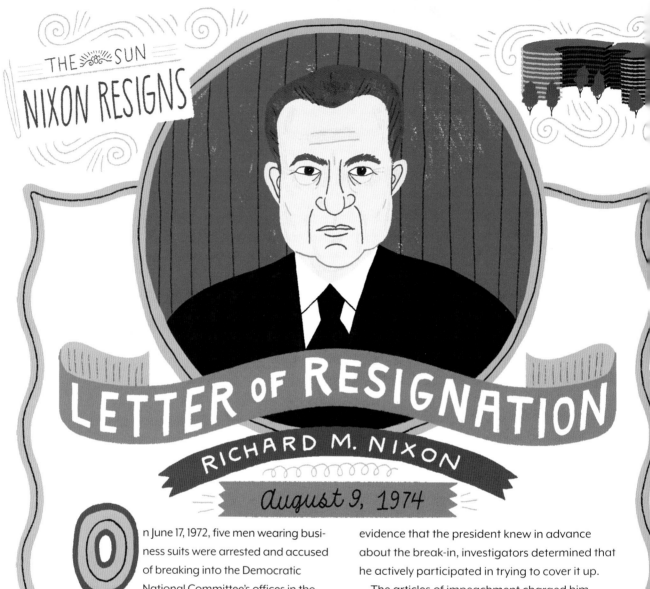

LETTER OF RESIGNATION

RICHARD M. NIXON

August 9, 1974

On June 17, 1972, five men wearing business suits were arrested and accused of breaking into the Democratic National Committee's offices in the Watergate building in Washington, D.C. They were wearing rubber gloves and had money stashed in their pockets. They were quickly identified as operatives for the Committee to Re-elect the President, and this was the beginning of what became known as Watergate scandal—the mother of all "-gates."

In late July, the House Judiciary Committee voted to adopt three articles of impeachment against President Richard M. Nixon because of his role in the scandal. Although there was no evidence that the president knew in advance about the break-in, investigators determined that he actively participated in trying to cover it up.

The articles of impeachment charged him with obstructing justice, misusing his powers, violating his oath of office, and refusing to produce material the committee had requested. Realizing that the House would almost certainly vote to impeach, Nixon wrote to Secretary of State Henry Kissinger, resigning the presidency. With this letter, he became the first president to resign. An orderly transfer of power occurred as Vice President Gerald Ford assumed the presidency.

LETTER OF RESIGNATION

THE WHITE HOUSE

WASHINGTON

August 9, 1974

Dear Mr. Secretary:

I hereby resign the Office of President of the
United States.

Sincerely,

[signature: Richard Nixon]

11.35 AM

HK

The Honorable Henry A. Kissinger
The Secretary of State
Washington, D.C. 20520

President Nixon, seated at his desk, announced his resignation on August 8, 1974. Nixon is the only American president to resign his office—doing so under the threat of impeachment—and to accept a pardon for wrongdoings in the Oval Office.

This 1973 photo shows Bob Woodward (left) and Carl Bernstein (right), two young reporters for *The Washington Post.* Their investigations of the Watergate case and President Nixon's role in it helped bring Watergate to the attention of the American people.

AUTHOR

California-born Richard M. Nixon (1913–1994) was the thirty-seventh president of the United States. Elected vice president in 1952, he served two terms under Republican president Dwight D. Eisenhower. In 1960 Nixon narrowly lost the presidential race to Democrat John F. Kennedy but won it in 1968, defeating Vice President Hubert Humphrey. Nixon had achieved several important breakthroughs in foreign policy, including opening relations with China and ending the Vietnam War.

After the Watergate scandal and his subsequent resignation, he spent much of the rest of his life rebuilding his reputation. He published a memoir in 1978, and later founded a political think tank.

RESPONSE

When Gerald Ford was sworn in as president on August 9, 1974, Americans were relieved that the turmoil had ended. The new president himself summed up most of the public's feelings best. Said Ford, "The long nightmare is over." The behavior that led to Nixon's leaving in disgrace had the effect of increasing the public's mistrust of politicians, while it elevated the role of a free press and of investigative journalists, who had exposed the crime. For many, the most important aspect of the Watergate scandal was the peaceful transfer of power that followed it. The Constitution and the institutions of the American government had passed a major test.

A month later, Ford granted Nixon a full pardon so that the nation could move on. But the pardon sparked its own controversy. Many Americans wanted Nixon to be prosecuted. Others did not want a former president in jail even if he was guilty. Still others felt that if he was innocent—Nixon had resigned before an impeachment trial could be held—then a pardon was an unfair stain on his reputation.

President Nixon addressed his resignation letter to the Secretary of State because he was following a 1792 act of Congress that established procedures for federal officials resigning from office.

Up to the last minute, President Nixon did not want to resign. But Republican leaders in Congress informed him that a majority of senators would vote for his impeachment.

During the Watergate scandal, President Nixon went on television and announced, "I am not a crook."

TEAR DOWN THIS WALL

RONALD W. REAGAN

June 12, 1987

President Ronald Reagan visited Berlin in June 1987 to celebrate the 750th anniversary of the founding of the city. Standing in front of the Brandenburg Gate, near the spot where President Kennedy delivered his "Ich bin ein Berliner" speech in 1961 (see p. 156), he issued a challenge to the Soviet leader, Mikhail Gorbachev, to "tear down" the Berlin Wall, perhaps the world's most visible symbol of the Cold War, and of the division between the two superpowers. Reagan told the West German crowd that prosperity was the hallmark of democracy and freedom, whereas the Communist Soviet system had resulted in widespread poverty and technological backwardness.

Reagan's speech proved prescient. In November 1989, the East German authorities allowed its citizens to leave East Berlin for the West, triggering a flood of defections into West Berlin and beyond. Families and friends were reunited in a joyful outpouring of emotion. East and West Germany were officially reunited in October 1990 under the West German government, and the dismantling of the wall was completed.

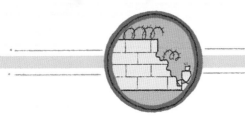

TEAR DOWN THIS WALL

Behind me stands a wall that encircles the free sectors of this city, part of a vast system of barriers that divides the entire continent of Europe. From the Baltic, south, those barriers cut across Germany in a gash of barbed wire, concrete, dog runs, and guardtowers [sic]. Farther south, there may be no visible, no obvious wall. But there remain armed guards and checkpoints all the same–still a restriction on the right to travel, still an instrument to impose upon ordinary men and women the will of a totalitarian state. Yet it is here in Berlin where the wall emerges most clearly; here, cutting across your city, where the news photo and the television screen have imprinted this brutal division of a continent upon the mind of the world. Standing before the Brandenburg Gate, every man is a German, separated from his fellow men. Every man is a Berliner, forced to look upon a scar. . . .

In the 1950s, Khrushchev predicted: "We will bury you." But in the West today, we see a free world that has achieved a level of prosperity and well-being unprecedented in all human history. In the Communist world, we see failure, technological backwardness, declining standards of health, even want of the most basic kind—too little food. Even today, the Soviet Union still cannot feed itself. After these four decades, then, there stands before the entire world one great and inescapable conclusion: Freedom leads to prosperity. Freedom replaces the ancient hatreds among the nations with comity and peace. Freedom is the victor. . . .

And now the Soviets themselves may, in a limited way, be coming to understand the importance of freedom. We hear much from Moscow about a new policy of reform and openness. Some political prisoners have been released. Certain foreign news broadcasts are no longer being jammed. Some economic enterprises have been permitted to operate with greater freedom from state control. Are these the beginnings of profound changes in the Soviet state? Or are they token gestures, intended to raise false hopes in the West, or to strengthen the Soviet system without changing it? We welcome change and openness; for we believe that freedom and security go together, that the advance of human liberty can only strengthen the cause of world peace. . . .

There is one sign the Soviets can make that would be unmistakable, that would advance dramatically the cause of freedom and peace. General Secretary Gorbachev, if you seek peace, if you seek prosperity for the Soviet Union and Eastern Europe, if you seek liberalization: Come here to this gate! Mr. Gorbachev, open this gate! Mr. Gorbachev, tear down this wall! ★

After World War II, Berlin, the capital of Germany was divided among the four victorious powers (see p. 156). But the United States, Great Britain, and France quickly grew suspicious of the intentions of the Soviet Union, and vice-versa. The three western powers governed West Berlin, which was completely surrounded by Soviet-governed East Berlin to the east and by the rest of East Germany to the north, south, and west.

Almost immediately, East German citizens began an exodus into West Berlin and then into West Germany, Europe, and beyond. It is estimated that between the late 1940s and 1961, 3.5 million East Germans fled to the West.

The Soviet-backed East German government responded to the enormous loss of its citizenry by beginning construction on the Berlin Wall in August 1961, calling it an "Anti-Fascist Protection Rampart"; most of the world saw it as a government imprisoning its own people.

By the time it was completed, the 12-foot-high wall—eventually fortified with barbed wire, heavily armed sentry towers, trip-wires, anti-vehicle trenches, and a 100-yard-wide "death strip" on the East German side—stretched for nearly 100 miles, surrounding West Berlin. Thirty miles of the wall ran down the heart of the city, splitting it from East Berlin.

Between 1961 and 1989, roughly 5,000 people managed to escape over, under, or through the wall. Escapees were resourceful: some fled by zip-wire, others by tightrope, still others via sewers or tunnels dug under the wall. One man drove an armored vehicle through the wall.

Western authorities estimate that East German security forces killed 137 people during escape attempts. Many more died in related accidents, such as jumping from windows, drowning, or by suffocating in collapsing tunnels.

Origins of the Cold War

At the end of World War II, defeated Germany was divided into four zones, each administered by one of the victorious Allies—Britain, France, the Soviet Union, and the United States. But mistrust between the Soviet Union and its wartime allies quickly sprang up. The Soviet leader, Joseph Stalin, believed that the United States had waited too long to enter the war, resulting in the deaths of millions of Soviet soldiers and civilians (the USSR suffered by far the largest number of deaths during World War II). The United States and its allies believed that Stalin was ruthlessly consolidating power at home and that he wanted to spread the Soviet system abroad. The two sides competed for any territory that was not clearly occupied by one side or the other at the end of the war.

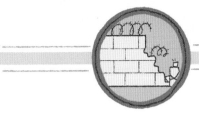

AUTHOR

Born into a poor Illinois family, Ronald Wilson Reagan (1911–2004) became a radio announcer and then, using his considerable charm and good looks, a Hollywood actor. As president of the Screen Actors Guild, Reagan's energy, wit, speech-making talents, and charisma began to be recognized. He used these skills to be elected Republican governor of California in 1966, and was reelected in 1970. Reagan lost in the 1976 Republican presidential primary to the incumbent, Gerald Ford, but won the 1980 presidential election in a landslide, carrying 44 of the 50 states. He was reelected in 1984, carrying 49 of the 50 states—among the most lopsided victories in American presidential history.

RESPONSE

President Ronald Reagan had gambled that a military buildup by the United States would push the Soviets, whom he believed to be more economically stressed than was commonly believed, to the breaking point. His speech at the Brandenburg Gate was a triumphant moment for him, as it marked the beginning of the end of the Cold War and what many regarded as vindication of his judgment.

Reagan was a highly appealing personality and a gifted speech-maker. He appeared to be a man of principle and conviction, making many Americans feel protected, secure, and proud of their country; others felt he was unsympathetic to the plight of the poor, opposing labor unions in favor of corporate interests and gutting the social safety net in favor of an unnecessarily large military buildup. Although the economy exploded during his presidency he left the United States with an enormous national debt, in some measure because of the military expansion he used as a tool to get the Soviets to the bargaining table.

Reagan's deep support of the military also led to the biggest scandal of his administration, the Iran-Contra affair. It was discovered by journalists that the United States had been secretly selling weapons to Iran—a violation of its own policy—and using the proceeds to fund a covert anti-Communist war in Nicaragua.

During his acting years, Ronald Reagan appeared in more than 50 films. One of his most beloved roles was his portrayal of football player George Gipp in *Knute Rockne–All American* (1940).

When Reagan was reelected in 1984, he won more votes than any previous president.

Ronald Reagan was sixty-nine years old when he was inaugurated, making him at that time the oldest president to be sworn into office. He was seventy-seven when he left office in 1988.

Reagan's nickname was The Great Communicator because he was able to clearly state his key issues. He made complex political and economic issues understandable to the American people.

In November, 1994, Ronald Reagan was diagnosed with Alzheimer's disease. He withdrew from public life until his death in 2004.

WOMEN'S RIGHTS ARE HUMAN RIGHTS

SPEECH AT THE
UNITED NATIONS CONFERENCE on WOMEN

HILLARY RODHAM CLINTON

September 5, 1995

Hillary Rodham Clinton, then known only as the wife of President William Jefferson Clinton, journeyed to China to address participants at the Fourth World Conference on Women, held in Beijing. Mrs. Clinton was the head of the U.S. delegation. In her remarks, Mrs. Clinton strongly supported the rights of women everywhere, equating women's rights with human rights. Clinton acknowledged the unequal status of women in the United States before proceeding to address the plight of women in war zones and in oppressive societies in which practices such as rape and genital mutilation are tolerated.

SPEECH AT THE UN CONFERENCE

. . . At this very moment, as we sit here, women around the world are giving birth, raising children, cooking meals, washing clothes, cleaning houses, planting crops, working on assembly lines, running companies, and running countries.

Women are also dying from diseases that should have been prevented or treated; they are watching their children succumb to malnutrition caused by poverty and economic deprivation; they are being denied the right to go to school by their own fathers and brothers; they are being forced into prostitution, and they are being barred from the ballot box and the bank-lending office.

Those of us with the opportunity to be here have the responsibility to speak for those who could not.

As an American, I want to speak up for women in my own country—women who are raising children on the minimum wage, women who can't afford health care or child care, women whose lives are threatened by violence, including violence in their own homes.

I want to speak up for mothers who are fighting for good schools, safe neighborhoods, clean air and clean airwaves . . . for older women, some of them widows, who have raised their families and now find that their skills and life experiences are not valued in the workplace . . . for women who are working all night as nurses, hotel clerks, and fast food chefs so that they can be at home during the day with their kids . . . and for women everywhere who simply don't have enough time to do everything they are called upon to do each day.

Speaking to you today, I speak for them, just as each of us speaks for women around the world who are denied the chance to go to school, or see a doctor, or own property, or have a say about the direction of their lives, simply because they are women.

The truth is that most women around the world work both inside and outside the home, usually by necessity.

We need to understand that there is no formula for how women should lead their lives. That is why we must respect the choices that each woman makes for herself and her family. Every woman deserves the chance to realize her God-given potential.

We must also recognize that women will never gain full dignity until their human rights are respected and protected.

Our goals for this conference, to strengthen families and societies by empowering women to take greater control over their own destinies, cannot be fully achieved unless all governments—here and around the world—accept their responsibility to protect and promote internationally recognized human rights.

The international community has long acknowledged—and recently affirmed at Vienna—that both women and men are entitled to a range of protections and personal freedoms, from the right of personal security to the right to determine freely the number and spacing of the children they bear.

No one should be forced to remain silent for fear of religious or political persecution, arrest, abuse or torture.

Tragically, women are most often the ones whose human rights are violated. Even in the late 20th century, the rape of women continues to be used as an instrument of armed conflict. Women and children make up a large majority of the world's refugees. And when women are excluded from the political process, they become even more vulnerable to abuse.

I believe that, on the eve of a new millennium, it is time to break our silence. It is time for us to say here in Beijing, and the world to hear, that it is no longer acceptable to discuss women's rights as separate from human rights.

These abuses have continued because, for too long, the history of women has been a history of silence. Even today, there are those who are trying to silence our words.

The voices of this conference and of the women at Hairou [Chinese city where women's rights delegates were also meeting] must be heard loud and clear.

It is a violation of human rights when babies are denied food, or drowned, or suffocated, or their spines broken, simply because they are girls.

It is a violation of human rights when women and girls are sold into the slavery of prostitution.

It is a violation of human rights when women are doused with gasoline, set on fire and burned to death because their marriage dowries are deemed too small.

It is a violation of human rights when individual women are raped in their own communities and when thousands of women are subjected to rape as a tactic or prize of war.

It is a violation of human rights when a leading cause of death worldwide among women ages 14 to 44 is the violence they are subjected to in their own homes.

It is a violation of human rights when young girls are brutalized by the painful and degrading practice of genital mutilation.

It is a violation of human rights when women are denied the right to plan their own families, and that includes being forced to have abortions or being sterilized against their will.

If there is one message that echoes forth from this conference, it is that human rights are women's rights . . . And women's rights are human rights.

Let us not forget that among those rights are the right to speak freely. And the right to be heard.

Women must enjoy the right to participate fully in the social and political lives of their countries if we want freedom and democracy to thrive and endure.

It is indefensible that many women in non-governmental organizations who wished to participate in this conference have not been able to attend—or have been prohibited from fully taking part.

Let me be clear. Freedom means the right of people to assemble, organize, and debate openly. It means respecting the views of those who may disagree with the views of their governments. It means not taking citizens away from their loved ones and jailing them, mistreating them, or denying them their freedom or dignity because of the peaceful expression of their ideas and opinions.

In my country, we recently celebrated the 75th anniversary of women's suffrage. It took 150 years after the signing of our Declaration of Independence for women to win the right to vote. It took 72 years of organized struggle on the part of many courageous women and men.

It was one of America's most divisive philosophical wars. But it was also a bloodless war. Suffrage was achieved without a shot fired.

We also have been reminded, in V-J Day observances last weekend, of the good that comes when men and women join together to combat the forces of tyranny and build a better world.

We have seen peace prevail in most places for a half century. We have avoided another world war.

But we have not solved older, deeply rooted problems that continue to diminish the potential of half the world's population.

Now it is time to act on behalf of women everywhere.

If we take bold steps to better the lives of women, we will be taking bold steps to better the lives of children and families too. Families rely on mothers and wives for emotional support and care; families rely on women for labor in the home; and increasingly, families rely on women for income needed to raise healthy children and care for other relatives.

As long as discrimination and inequities remain so common-place around the world—as long as girls and women are valued less, fed less, fed last, overworked, underpaid, not schooled and subjected to violence in and out of their homes—the potential of the human family to create a peaceful, prosperous world will not be realized.

Let this conference be our—and the world's—call to action.

And let us heed the call so that we can create a world in which every woman is treated with respect and dignity, every boy and girl is loved and cared for equally, and every family has the hope of a strong and stable future.

Thank you very much. God's blessings on you, your work and all who benefit from it.

Women of all nations attended the U.N. Conference on Women. Shown here are delegates from Muslim countries.

First Lady Hillary Rodham Clinton addressed the U.N. Conference on Women on September 5, 1995.

The United Nations' emblem incorporates a map of the globe surrounded by two olive branches, the traditional symbol of peace.

Women from 180 countries attended the conference.

During Mrs. Clinton's speech, her audience showed their approval by thumping desks as well as by applauding.

In 1979 the United Nations issued the Convention on the Elimination of All Forms of Discrimination against Women. The guidelines put forth at that meeting are often described as a Bill of Rights for women and have now been ratified by 160 countries.

Some critics, disturbed by China's poor record on human rights, criticized Clinton and the U.S. delegation for for participating in a conference held in Beijing.

AUTHOR

Born to a middle-class family in Chicago, Illinois, Hillary Rodham Clinton (b. 1947) served as U.S. Senator from New York from 2001 until she was sworn in as Secretary of State under President Barack Obama (who had defeated her in the 2008 Democratic primaries) in 2009. She ran unsuccessfully as the Democratic candidate for president in 2016 against Donald Trump. At the time of the Beijing conference, she was the First Lady of the United States. She had met President Bill Clinton when they were both students at Yale law school. Throughout her career—as First Lady, senator, and Secretary of State—Mrs. Clinton has been an advocate for the rights of women and children.

RESPONSE

Clinton's speech was positively received by the delegation in Beijing. The conference adopted the Beijing Declaration and the Platform for Action, considered by many still to be the key global policy document on gender equality. The Declaration set goals and strategies for addressing issues like poverty among women, reproductive health, and violence against women. The presence of the first lady of the United States had brought additional media attention to the event. Religious leaders such as Mother Theresa, who spoke at the conference, condemned some of the Declaration's conclusions, particularly those on abortion and women's reproductive rights.

Addressing the 2016 Democratic Convention after being named the party's candidate for president, Clinton tied her work on behalf of women to her personal story. "On the very day my mother was born in Chicago," she told the crowd, "Congress was passing the 19th amendment to the constitution [see p. 124]. That amendment finally gave women the right to vote. And I really wish my mother could be here tonight . . . I wish she could see her daughter become the Democratic Party's nominee."

ADDRESS TO THE NATION
ON THE SEPTEMBER 11 ATTACKS

GEORGE W. BUSH

September 11, 2001

The nation had never experienced such a dramatic and devastating terrorist attack on its own soil before September 11, 2001. President George W. Bush had been in office for less than a year, and he now faced the biggest test of leadership of his presidency.

He had to inform and reassure the nation, and express empathy for the terrible personal losses that had affected so many people. He had to tell people how the government would answer to these attacks, and show the rest of the world how the United States would respond to such a bold and calculated act. Perhaps most importantly, he had to set the tone for how the nation should behave.

His speech marks an important crossroads in America's leadership in the world and in its ongoing struggle to find the proper balance between national security and civil liberties.

ADDRESS TO THE NATION

Good evening.

Today, our fellow citizens, our way of life, our very freedom came under attack in a series of deliberate and deadly terrorist acts.

The victims were in airplanes or in their offices – secretaries, businessmen and women, military and federal workers. Moms and dads. Friends and neighbors.

Thousands of lives were suddenly ended by evil, despicable acts of terror.

The pictures of airplanes flying into buildings, fires burning, huge structures collapsing, have filled us with disbelief, terrible sadness and a quiet, unyielding anger.

These acts of mass murder were intended to frighten our nation into chaos and retreat. But they have failed. Our country is strong. A great people has been moved to defend a great nation.

Terrorist attacks can shake the foundations of our biggest buildings, but they cannot touch the foundation of America. These acts shatter steel, but they cannot dent the steel of American resolve.

America was targeted for attack because we're the brightest beacon for freedom and opportunity in the world. And no one will keep that light from shining.

Today, our nation saw evil, the very worst of human nature, and we responded with the best of America, with the daring of our rescue workers, with the caring for strangers and neighbors who came to give blood and help in any way they could.

Immediately following the first attack, I implemented our government's emergency response plans. Our military is powerful, and it's prepared. Our emergency teams are working in New York City and Washington, D.C., to help with local rescue efforts.

Our first priority is to get help to those who have been injured and to take every precaution to protect our citizens at home and around the world from further attacks.

The functions of our government continue without interruption. Federal agencies in Washington which had to be evacuated today are reopening for essential personnel tonight and will be open for business tomorrow.

Our financial institutions remain strong, and the American economy will be open for business as well.

➤⟶

The search is underway for those who are behind these evil acts. I've directed the full resources for our intelligence and law enforcement communities to find those responsible and bring them to justice. We will make no distinction between the terrorists who committed these acts and those who harbor them.

I appreciate so very much the members of Congress who have joined me in strongly condemning these attacks. And on behalf of the American people, I thank the many world leaders who have called to offer their condolences and assistance.

America and our friends and allies join with all those who want peace and security in the world and we stand together to win the war against terrorism.

Tonight I ask for your prayers for all those who grieve, for the children whose worlds have been shattered, for all whose sense of safety and security has been threatened. And I pray they will be comforted by a power greater than any of us spoken through the ages in Psalm 23: "Even though I walk through the valley of the shadow of death, I fear no evil, for You are with me."

This is a day when all Americans from every walk of life unite in our resolve for justice and peace. America has stood down enemies before, and we will do so this time.

None of us will ever forget this day, yet we go forward to defend freedom and all that is good and just in our world.

Thank you. Good night and God bless America. ★

Gathered in a classroom at the Emma E. Booker Elementary School in Sarasota, FL, where he was speaking when the attacks occurred, President Bush speaks on the phone while Dan Bartlett (Deputy Assistant to the President) points to news footage of the attacks. Also shown (left to right): Deborah Loewer (Director of White House Situation Room) and Karl Rove (Senior Adviser).

Hijacked jets destroyed a section of the Pentagon in Washington, D.C. (below) and both towers of the World Trade Center in New York, NY, on September 11, 2001.

What Happened on 9/11?

On the crystal clear morning of September 11, 2001, a group of nineteen terrorists hijacked airplanes originating in three different U.S. cities shortly after takeoff. They used the four hijacked jets as missiles, perpetrating suicide attacks in three locations in the eastern United States, killing nearly 3,000 people. The attacks were planned and executed by members of al-Qaeda, a radical Islamic terrorist group led by the radicalized son of a wealthy Saudi Arabian family, Osama bin Laden.

Terrorists flew a fuel-laden jet into each of the two World Trade Center towers in New York City, igniting fireballs within the 110-story towers that led to their collapse, 29 minutes apart. Approximately 2,750 people lost their lives (the exact number is not known), including the passengers and crews on the airplanes. Tunnels and bridges into New York were closed, and the city was on virtual lockdown for several days. Smoldering fires burned for three months. Cleanup of the area, which contained toxic chemicals and human remains, took months. Rebuilding the site took many years.

A third jet was flown into the side of the Pentagon, in Arlington, Virginia, just outside of Washington, D.C. One hundred and eighty-nine people were killed in that attack. The section of the Pentagon that was destroyed in the attack was demolished and rebuilt in nine months. The final piece of limestone to be placed was one that was scarred and discolored from the attack.

The fourth jet crashed in a field near Shanksville, Pennsylvania, killing all 40 passengers and crew members aboard. Passengers, alerted by cell phone, banded together and fought the terrorists, thwarting them. The planned target of that jet remains unknown, but it is widely thought to have been the U.S. Capitol Building or the White House.

The twin towers had been attacked once before, when a truck bomb exploded in the parking garage of 2 World Trade Center in 1993, killing six and injuring 1,000.

An unidentifed firefighter walks away from the smouldering remains of the World Trade Center, known as Ground Zero. More than 400 firefighters and law enforcement officers were killed in the attacks.

President Bush prepares his speech about the attacks. From left to right: Condoleezza Rice (National Security Adviser); Karen Hughes (Counselor); Ari Fleischer (Press Secretary); Andy Card (Chief of Staff); and President Bush.

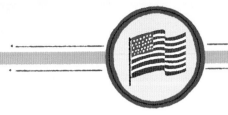

AUTHOR

The nation's 43rd president was born in New Haven, Connecticut, in 1946 and grew up in Midland and Houston, Texas. His grandfather, Prescott Bush, had been a U.S. Senator from Connecticut, and his father, George H. W. Bush, had been vice president under Ronald Reagan, and the 41st president of the United States. George W. was governor of Texas from 1995 until 2000, when he was elected to the Oval Office.

In response to the 9/11 attacks, President Bush introduced the USA Patriot Act, which eliminated certain civil and criminal legal protections in order to make it easier for investigators to detect, prevent, and prosecute acts of terrorism. The Patriot Act also created more comprehensive rules to prevent money laundering, which had been used to fund terrorism. Less than a month after 9/11, President Bush ordered the invasion of Afghanistan in an effort to root out al-Qaeda. This became the longest running war in U.S. history. In 2003, President Bush ordered U.S. troops to invade Iraq, which he said supported al-Qaeda and housed weapons of mass destruction, a charge that later proved to be false.

RESPONSE

President Bush's words helped the shaken nation understand the magnitude of what had happened on 9/11, offered solace to those who had suffered loss, and reassured people that the military might and preparedness of the United States would protect them. His words also served to reassure the financial markets and to let citizens and the world know that business—and life— would continue much as it had before the attacks, only with increased vigilance and new protective measures in place.

The nation was now on alert: a new era of terror had arrived, and no country, not even the United States, could afford to assume that it was safe. The balance between the need for heightened security and the rights of the individual to privacy and the presumption of innocence is an issue that continues to be debated.

President Bush confers with his staff via phone aboard *Air Force One*.

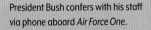

SPEECH ON RACE

BARACK OBAMA

March 18, 2008

Senator Barack Obama, who in 2008 was a Democratic candidate for President, addressed the issue of race in America in front a rapt audience at the Constitution Center in Philadelphia. The speech came several days after controversial remarks by the pastor of Obama's church in Chicago, the Reverend Jeremiah Wright, were publicized in the media. Many thought that Obama's candidacy, which promised racial unity, was in deep trouble.

Obama responded with this speech. He called slavery America's "original sin," and said that racism remains a part of the makeup of this country, causing a stubborn divide—a racial stalemate—to which both whites and blacks have contributed. Obama used his personal history to illustrate both the importance and the *possibility* of reconciling these racial differences, and called on members of both races to press forward together and face the economic and strategic challenges confronting America.

SPEECH ON RACE

I am the son of a black man from Kenya and a white woman from Kansas. I was raised with the help of a white grandfather who survived a Depression to serve in Patton's Army during World War II and a white grandmother who worked on a bomber assembly line at Fort Leavenworth while he was overseas. I've gone to some of the best schools in America and lived in one of the world's poorest nations. I am married to a black American who carries within her the blood of slaves and slaveowners — an inheritance we pass on to our two precious daughters. I have brothers, sisters, nieces, nephews, uncles and cousins of every race and every hue, scattered across three continents, and for as long as I live, I will never forget that in no other country on Earth is my story even possible.

It's a story that hasn't made me the most conventional of candidates. But it is a story that has seared into my genetic makeup the idea that this nation is more than the sum of its parts—that out of many, we are truly one. . . .

And yet . . . in the last couple of weeks . . . the discussion of race in this campaign has taken a particularly divisive turn.

On one end of the spectrum, we've heard the implication that my candidacy is somehow an exercise in affirmative action; that it's based solely on the desire of wide-eyed liberals to purchase racial reconciliation on the cheap. On the other end, we've heard my former pastor, Jeremiah Wright, use incendiary language to express views that have the potential not only to widen the racial divide, but views that denigrate both the greatness and the goodness of our nation, and that rightly offend white and black alike. . . .

I have already condemned, in unequivocal terms, the statements of Reverend Wright that have caused such controversy and, in some cases, pain. For some, nagging questions remain. Did I know him to be an occasionally fierce critic of American domestic and foreign policy? Of course. Did I ever hear him make remarks that could be considered controversial while I sat in the church? Yes. Did I strongly disagree with many of his political views? Absolutely—just as I'm sure many of you have heard remarks from your pastors, priests, or rabbis with which you strongly disagreed. . . .

. . . As imperfect as he may be, [Reverend Wright] has been like family to me. He strengthened my faith, officiated my wedding, and baptized my children. Not once in my conversations with him have I heard him talk about any ethnic group in derogatory terms, or treat whites with whom he interacted with anything but courtesy and respect. He contains within him the contradictions—the good and the bad—of the community that he has served diligently for so many years. . . .

. . . I can no more disown him than I can disown the black community. I can no more disown him than I can disown my white grandmother—a woman who helped raise me, a woman who sacrificed again and again for me, a woman who loves me as much as she loves anything in this world, but a woman who once confessed her fear of black men who passed her by on the street, and who on more than one occasion has uttered racial or ethnic stereotypes that made me cringe.

These people are a part of me. And they are part of America, this country that I love. . . .

The fact is that the comments that have been made and the issues that have surfaced over the last few weeks reflect the complexities of race in this country that we've never really worked through—a part of our union that we have not yet made perfect. And if we walk away now, if we simply retreat into our respective corners, we will never be able to come together and solve challenges like health care or education or the need to find good jobs for every American.

. . . We do not need to recite here the history of racial injustice in this country. But we do need to remind ourselves that so many of the disparities that exist between the African-American community and the larger American community today can be traced directly to inequalities passed on from an earlier generation that suffered under the brutal legacy of slavery and Jim Crow.

Segregated schools were and are inferior schools; we still haven't fixed them, 50 years after *Brown v. Board of Education*. And the inferior education they provided, then and now, helps explain the pervasive achievement gap between today's black and white students.

Legalized discrimination—where blacks were prevented, often through violence, from owning property, or loans were not granted to African-American business owners, or black homeowners could not access FHA mortgages, or blacks were excluded from unions or the police force or the fire department—meant that black families could not amass any meaningful wealth to bequeath to future generations. That history helps explain the wealth and income gap between blacks and whites, and the concentrated pockets of poverty that persist in so many of today's urban and rural communities.

A lack of economic opportunity among black men, and the shame and frustration that came from not being able to provide for one's family contributed to the erosion of black families—a problem that welfare policies for many years may have worsened. And the lack of basic services in so many urban black neighborhoods—parks for kids to play in, police walking the beat, regular garbage pickup, building code enforcement—all helped create a cycle of violence, blight and neglect that continues to haunt us. . . .

For all those who scratched and clawed their way to get a piece of the American Dream, there were many who didn't make it—those who were ultimately defeated, in one way or another, by discrimination. That legacy of defeat was passed on to future generations—those young men and, increasingly, young women who we see standing on street corners or languishing in our prisons, without hope or prospects for the future. Even for those blacks who did make it, questions of race and racism continue to define their worldview in fundamental ways. For the men and women of Reverend Wright's generation, the memories of humiliation and doubt and fear have not gone away; nor has the anger and the bitterness of those years. That anger may not get expressed in public, in front of white co-workers or white friends. But it does find voice in the barbershop or the beauty shop or around the kitchen table. . . .

And occasionally it finds voice in the church on Sunday morning, in the pulpit and in the pews. The fact that so many people are surprised to hear that anger in some of Reverend Wright's sermons simply reminds us of the old truism that the most segregated hour of American life occurs on Sunday morning. That anger is not always productive; indeed, all too often it distracts attention from solving real problems; it keeps us from squarely facing our own complicity within the African-American community in our condition, and prevents the African-American community from forging the alliances it needs to bring about real change. But the anger is real; it is powerful. And to simply wish it away, to condemn it without understanding its roots, only serves to widen the chasm of misunderstanding that exists between the races.

In fact, a similar anger exists within segments of the white community. Most working- and middle-class white Americans don't feel that they have been particularly privileged by their race. Their experience is the immigrant experience—as far as they're concerned, no one handed them anything. They built it from scratch. They've worked hard all their lives, many times only to see their jobs shipped overseas or their pensions dumped after a lifetime of labor. They are anxious about their futures, and they feel their dreams slipping away. And in an era of stagnant wages and global competition, opportunity comes to be seen as a zero sum game, in which your dreams come at my expense. So when they are told to bus their children to a school across town; when they hear an African-American is getting an advantage in landing a good job or a spot in a good college because of an injustice that they themselves never committed; when they're told that their fears about crime in urban neighborhoods are somehow prejudiced, resentment builds over time.

Like the anger within the black community, these resentments aren't always expressed in polite company. But they have helped shape the political landscape for at least a generation. Anger over welfare and affirmative action helped forge the Reagan Coalition. Politicians routinely exploited fears of crime for their own electoral ends. Talk show hosts and conservative commentators built entire careers unmasking bogus claims of racism while dismissing legitimate discussions of racial injustice and

→

inequality as mere political correctness or reverse racism.

Just as black anger often proved counterproductive, so have these white resentments distracted attention from the real culprits of the middle class squeeze—a corporate culture rife with inside dealing, questionable accounting practices and short-term greed; a Washington dominated by lobbyists and special interests; economic policies that favor the few over the many. And yet, to wish away the resentments of white Americans, to label them as misguided or even racist, without recognizing they are grounded in legitimate concerns—this too widens the racial divide and blocks the path to understanding.

This is where we are right now. It's a racial stalemate we've been stuck in for years. Contrary to the claims of some of my critics, black and white, I have never been so naïve as to believe that we can get beyond our racial divisions in a single election cycle, or with a single candidacy—particularly a candidacy as imperfect as my own.

But I have asserted a firm conviction—a conviction rooted in my faith in God and my faith in the American people—that, working together, we can move beyond some of our old racial wounds, and that in fact we have no choice if we are to continue on the path of a more perfect union. . . .

The profound mistake of Reverend Wright's sermons is not that he spoke about racism in our society. It's that he spoke as if our society was static; as if no progress had been made; as if this country—a country that has made it possible for one of his own members to run for the highest office in the land and build a coalition of white and black, Latino and Asian, rich and poor, young and old—is still irrevocably bound to a tragic past. But what we know—what we have seen—is that America can change. That is the true genius of this nation. What we have already achieved gives us hope—the audacity to hope—for what we can and must achieve tomorrow. . . .

I would not be running for President if I didn't believe with all my heart that this is what the vast majority of Americans want for this country. This union may never be perfect, but generation after generation has shown that it can always be perfected. And today, whenever I find myself feeling doubtful or cynical about this possibility, what gives me the most hope is the next generation—the young people whose attitudes and beliefs and openness to change have already made history in this election. ★

What Did Reverend Jeremiah Wright Say?

Reverend Wright was an adherent of black liberation theology, an activist Christian philosophy that took root in the 1960s, which asserted that God was intimately involved in the struggle for social justice, and wanted to eradicate poverty and bring freedom and liberation to the oppressed. In a sermon delivered September 18, 2001, Reverend Wright said that violence begets violence, and since America dropped bombs and supported governments overseas that violently oppressed their people, the terrorist attack on 9/11 should have been expected. "America's chickens are coming home to roost," he said, paraphrasing Malcolm X. In a 2003 sermon, Wright had said that blacks had a right to be angry about slavery and their continued mistreatment, making perhaps his most inflammatory statement. "No, no, no, not God Bless America," he said. "God damn America—that's in the Bible—for killing innocent people. God damn America, for treating our citizens as less than human."

Delivering a major address at the Democratic National Convention at the National Constitution Center in Philadelphia, presidential candidate Sen. Barack Obama rejected the controversial statements by his pastor Rev. Jeremiah Wright and talked about the need for unity.

Students from Baltimore colleges and high schools march in protest chanting '"Justice for Freddie Gray'" on April 29, 2015, in Baltimore, Maryland. Gray died of an injury in police custody after an arrest.